ADVANCE PRAISE

Lak brings his years of real-world experience building startups and new businesses inside large companies into this book, and I am certain that any founder, entrepreneur, or executive will benefit greatly from reading it. I know from personal experience that there are lessons to be learned from startups, even for a large, global business such as ours. Through my thought partnership with Lak, I have transferred many of these startup lessons into Siemens with favorable outcomes.

—DR. ROLAND BUSCH, President and CEO, Siemens AG

Anticipate Failure is a rare look into the causes of business failure and why so many leaders don't adequately address them until it's too late. Through plenty of in-depth case studies, the book provides readers with a proven roadmap for anticipating the most common points of business failure and then navigating their way through them.

—GRAZIA VITTADINI, CTO at Airbus

Insightful, thought-provoking, and eminently practical. Lak Ananth has crafted a powerful guidebook rooted in the philosophy that the key to safeguarding success is a deep understanding of the drivers of failure. A rewarding journey through fascinating case studies, powerful concepts, and constructive coaching, *Anticipate Failure* is a valuable addition to the entrepreneurial tool kit.

—RON ADNER, Leverone Memorial Professor, Tuck School of Business at Dartmouth College, Author of *The Wide Lens* and *Winning the Right Game*

When I built my own businesses, I had the good fortune to be able to gain insights from my strong personal network of entrepreneurs, along with great investors who offered their timely guidance. They helped me take advantage of opportunities and recover from the inevitable failures. But what if you don't have a network to draw on for advice as you grow your business? In *Anticipate Failure*, Lak Ananth coaches readers through the most common sources of failure, providing tremendously valuable advice. I wish I had a book like this when I founded my own startups—it would have been a huge benefit to me, my customers, and my companies.

—BILL TRENCHARD, Partner, First Round Capital

In his book *Anticipate Failure*, Lak Ananth addresses a topic that is of critical importance to every entrepreneur, which is to expect and prepare for failure when starting a new venture. As veteran company founders know all too well, it's not a question of if failure will arrive—it's when. A methodical framework such as mine, coupled with Lak's book, will go a long way to help any entrepreneur get their venture off the ground, find their way past failure points, and get to ultimate success.

—MOHIT ARON, Founder & CEO, Cohesity, Co-Founder & CTO, Nutanix

Anticipate Failure, written by Lak Ananth—CEO of venture firm Next47 and one of INSEAD's senior alumni in the VC space—guides entrepreneurs through the most common sources of failure, and in turn, offers valuable advice that is rare to come by. Entrepreneurs and business builders will truly appreciate this book and the tools it offers to navigate failure and ultimately find the success they so richly deserve.

—CLAUDIA ZEISBERGER, Professor of Entrepreneurship at INSEAD, Author of *Mastering Private Equity: Transformation via Venture Capital, Minority Investments & Buyouts*

Lak Ananth's book *Anticipate Failure* paints a comprehensive and well-illustrated picture of the kinds of failure that can harm a business and its journey to success. I recognize a lot of sennder's challenges and failures in the book, and I know a lot of founders, including myself, will probably find Lak's insights very useful for their own journey.

—DAVID NOTHACKER, Co-Founder and CEO, sennder

Business failure is painful. By looking fearlessly at the possibilities of failure, entrepreneurs can learn to avoid them. In his excellent and timely book *Anticipate Failure*, Lak Ananth teaches the tricks to turn risks into opportunities and mistakes into learning experiences.

—MARTEN MICKOS, CEO, HackerOne

After years of working directly with some of today's most successful businesses and their founders and executives, Lak Ananth has distilled the lessons he has learned in this book—valuable lessons that will encourage European founders, corporations, and governments to aim high and build great organizations.

—DR. GERHARD CROMME, Former Chairman of Supervisory Board at Siemens AG and ThyssenKrupp AG

Founders—myself included—are often pathologically optimistic. We assume we'll succeed and thus don't give failure enough thought. In his book *Anticipate Failure*, Lak Ananth persuades through hard-earned lessons conveyed with wit and warmth that we should channel our optimism toward actively identifying and avoiding failure modes. It struck me as odd that I hadn't seen a book organized like this before —it's pretty obvious this book should exist. Now it does, and I believe it will help the next generation of entrepreneurs build more successful companies with better odds.

—JOHN BEATTY, Co-Founder and CEO, Clover

As a company founder, I have learned firsthand that failure is always waiting patiently just around the corner. The problem is that you're never sure which direction it's going to come from and when it will arrive. In *Anticipate Failure*, Lak Ananth explains that failure is common—it's something that every business builder can and should anticipate. And, with the right tools at their disposal—which Lak provides in his groundbreaking book—they can work through failure and get to the other side stronger than ever.

—WILL CHAN, Co-Founder of Cloud.com and Rancher Labs

Darkest Hour is one of my two favorite movies, *The Post* being the other. A Winston Churchill quote (from *Darkest Hour*) that has had a profound impact on my life goes like this: *"Success is not final, failure is not fatal. It's the courage to continue that counts."* Lak's book, especially the final chapter, reminds me of that anti-fragile mindset that I try to inculcate in my post-COVID life, including with my children, every day.

—DHEERAJ PANDEY, Chairman & CEO, DevRev

In his book *Anticipate Failure*, Lak Ananth provides readers with an essential roadmap to the most common sources of business failure. Lak offers the benefit of his years of experience working with startups to coach readers through failure and to the success they work so hard to attain. By helping your people *Anticipate Failure* and then providing them with the tools they need to work their way through it, you will unleash their great human potential to reinvent the companies for which they work.

– JIM HAGEMANN SNABE, Chairman of Supervisory Board at Siemens AG and A. P. Moller Maersk, Former Co-CEO, SAP AG

Anticipate Failure is a rare look into the causes of business failure. Packed with in-depth case studies and interviews with some of today's most successful startup founders and entrepreneurs, the book provides readers with tools to anticipate the most common points of business failure and provides insights on how to navigate through them. The stories Lak Ananth tells are both entertaining and eye-opening.

–GREG MARK, Chairman & Founder, Markforged

When embarking upon a journey where the stakes are high and odds of success are low, having a guide who knows where the land mines are buried is worth much more than a treasure map. In *Anticipate Failure*, Lak Ananth, through his personal journey, guides us on how to identify and avoid such land mines, empowering us to each forge our own path toward ultimate success.

–RENEN HALLAK, CEO & Founder, VAST Data

In *Anticipate Failure*, Lak Ananth provides us with the benefit of his many years of experience helping business builders launch and grow companies. The book is full of current examples of business and interviews with some of today's most successful founders and executives. Putting the lessons contained in this book to work in your own business can help you find success.

–N. KUMAR, Vice Chairman of the Sanmar Group, Former President CII

ANTICIPATE FAILURE

IDEAPRESS
PUBLISHING

Printed in the United States.

Ideapress Publishing | www.ideapresspublishing.com

Cover Design: Lindy Martin, Faceout Studio
Interior Design: Paul Nielsen, Faceout Studio

Cataloging-in-Publication Data is on file with the Library of Congress.

ISBN: 978-1-64687-072-1

Special Sales
Ideapress Books are available at a special discount for bulk purchases for sales promotions and premiums, or for use in corporate training programs. Special editions, including personalized covers, a custom foreword, corporate imprints, and bonus content, are also available.

ANTICIPATE FAILURE

THE ENTREPRENEUR'S GUIDE TO
NAVIGATING UNCERTAINTY, AVOIDING DISASTER, AND BUILDING A SUCCESSFUL BUSINESS

BY

LAK ANANTH

IDEAPRESS
PUBLISHING

WASHINGTON, D.C.

To my parents, wife, son, and family:
Everything I am is the sum total of
everything you've done for me.

My success is your success.

CONTENTS

FOREWORD

Failure is something that everyone experiences throughout our careers and lives. Whether or not we like it—most of us don't—it's something we must learn in order to build resilience and thrive. The key is not to fear failure, but to anticipate it, prepare for it, do everything in your power to resolve the problems that led to it, and learn lessons that will help you and your team do better in the future.

Unfortunately, many organizations and the people who work in them are afraid of failure, and for good reason. They are embarrassed by it, they are punished for it, and they may even lose their jobs over it. In my experience, this is not the pathway for long-term organizational success. We must be open to failure and delve into its root causes instead of avoiding it, hiding it, and hoping that it will go away.

How can we do that?

I believe that it's up to leaders to create an environment that does not punish their people for failure, but instead brings failure into the open so it can be resolved before small failures become large ones. The longer that small failures are ignored or concealed, the greater the probability that a much more serious failure will be the inevitable outcome. When that is the case, your job will be made that much more difficult if not impossible.

Accomplishing this requires openness from the top to the bottom of the organization. Often managers are not open to accepting failures or problems, and their people who experience them are reluctant to admit them. If you're not open, how can you improve? I believe you cannot. You must give in to failure, pick yourself up, and try again. In sports, when you do something new—hitting a tennis serve or kicking a soccer ball into the goal—at the beginning you think, "I will never get it." But if you try it again and again, your muscle memory finally comes into play, and you learn the skill. The more you practice it, the better you get.

It's the same in business. When you are learning a new skill, it may seem daunting at first, and you may fall down a few times along the way. But if you keep at it and don't give up, you eventually will master it.

One of the most important things that a good leader does is pick the right people for the right things to do, and we at Siemens got it right with Lak. I first met Lak in 2016, when he interviewed for the role of CEO at Next47. In our initial conversation, I found Lak to be a strategic thinker on business building with a clear point of view and a brilliant mind. We asked Lak to lead Next47, and he has built the business from scratch into a world-class, global venture firm. The venture capital business is really special, and not everyone can do the job. As a venture investor, you need not only to understand business-building principles, but also to be a trusted partner and coach to company founders. In addition, to build a global venture firm as Lak has done, you must be a well-rounded leader with a lot of experience in different disciplines.

Lak brings his years of real-world experience building startups and new businesses inside large companies into this book, and I am certain that any founder, entrepreneur, or executive will benefit greatly from reading it. I know from personal experience that there are lessons to be learned from startups, even for a large, global business such as ours. Through my thought partnership with Lak, I have transferred many of these startup lessons into Siemens with favorable outcomes. I am able to do this because the basic principles are always there: Learn what customers really need. Focus on what you're good at. Excel at execution. Of course, once you scale up from a one hundred–person organization to a ten thousand–person organization, there are other things to consider, but the basic principles endure.

By putting the powerful lessons you'll read in this book to work, you are making a commitment to your long-term success. Keep in mind that the road to success is always going to be filled with potholes, and failure is waiting for you around every corner. But taking on these obstacles and solving them is the best way to find sustainable growth and success in any endeavor.

With this book in hand, you have everything you need to anticipate failure and succeed—now and in the future. I wish you well on your journey.

—Dr. Roland Busch,
President and CEO, Siemens AG

INTRODUCTION

O traveler, why worry about sorrow?
Happiness is but a transient shadow that comes and goes.
Sorrow is our companion.

The quote above is an excerpt from *"Raahi Manwa Dukh Ki Chinta,"* a Hindi song with music composed by the duo Laxmikant-Pyarelal and featured in the 1964 film *Dosti*. I feel a deep personal connection to this song and the lyrics for two reasons.

First, soon after I was born, my parents chose my name—Lakshmikanth, or Lak for short—in honor of the song's composer. Second, the lyrics tell us not to be afraid of sorrow because sorrow is our friend and companion. It's happiness that comes and goes as it will. Similarly, in business, we shouldn't be afraid of failure because failure is our friend and companion. Success, on the other hand, comes and goes—it's not reliable, and it's not guaranteed. Once you understand that, then you know that your job as a business leader is to anticipate the failure that is always just around the corner and find ways to succeed, build, and sustain that success in every possible way.

I came to the United States from India in 1994, at the cusp of the Internet era. My plan was to find my way to Manhattan—the Big City—and enroll in graduate school. However, in all my naivete, I truly didn't know the difference between Manhattan, Kansas, and Manhattan, New York—America is America, right?

I ended up in Manhattan, Kansas.

My father emptied his bank account to pay for the plane ticket and to give me the $200 I had in my pocket when I arrived in the United States. This was a fortune for my family. I vividly remember getting off the plane in Chicago to catch my connecting flight to Kansas City. I stopped at a McDonald's in the terminal and purchased a small Coke for 49 cents. It was the first money I spent in the United States.

When I got off the plane in Kansas City, I looked around and wondered, "Where are all the skyscrapers? Where are all the cars and subway trains and hustle and bustle? Why is the bus driver waxing poetic about Flint Hills?"

I soon discovered that there is more than one Manhattan in the United States, but I decided to stay anyway, enrolling at Kansas State University. My advisor, Dr. Medhat Morcos, kindly footed my tuition for the first semester and supported me through a research assistantship.

I had the great fortune to move to California's Silicon Valley in 1997. Netscape had just gone public, and I had a chance to be an engineer and work in startups that were a part of the explosive growth of the dot-com bubble. I found my way to a venture firm, then Cisco, and then Hewlett-Packard. Finally, in 2016, I became CEO of Next47, a global venture firm.

My focus has always been in technology, and I have worked with many talented founders and executives throughout my career as an engineer, product manager, customer account manager, acquisition professional, and venture investor. Every day I feel fortunate to lead Next47 and to meet and work with remarkable people who are building amazing companies. We are in a golden era where entrepreneurship is celebrated and practiced at a high level globally. Whether we are in Bangalore or Beijing, Berlin or Munich, Palo Alto or Paris or Tel Aviv, the founders we talk with are equally ambitious and talented, and they are accomplishing great things.

One of the experiences that crystalized my approach to venture investing was participating in the Kauffman Fellows program—a two-year leadership development program for venture capitalists. The program was born in an era when founders were undervalued, and it was hard for them to get funding. The remarkable things that founders did and the sacrifices they made to build something were not always appreciated by venture investors. The lasting belief I took away from my experience as a Kauffman Fellow was the ethos to put founders first when they choose us to be their investment partner and to do everything in our power to earn and keep their trust. Our job as investors is to empower founders and help them succeed. Sometimes that means, to paraphrase English poet John Milton, serving as we stand and wait.

We at Next47 have built a firm that serves founders. We have the expertise, experience, and resources to help them. We meet with entrepreneurs all around the world, learn about their vision for the future, and become partners in their journey.

Next47 would not have been possible without the great partnership that we've had with Dr. Roland Busch, CEO of Siemens. When I interviewed for the Next47 CEO job and met Roland for the first time, I realized that we were kindred spirits. We both love big challenges. Roland has always appreciated meeting great people and helping them become successful—that is his fundamental philosophy and approach. At the same time, he doesn't always operate at the one hundred thousand–foot level. Roland is a builder at heart—he can get his hands dirty and work at any level. He has been a role model to me on how to be a great leader—digging into the details when necessary, wholeheartedly trusting and supporting his top talent, always optimistic, and quietly inspiring.

Roland has created the space for us to build Next47 and reach more founders. I am grateful for my partnership with him and for his commitment and willingness to understand how the world of startups works, to have an open mind, and to welcome founders into the family.

Why write a book about failure? Let me share the backstory. In 2005, while I was pursuing my MBA at INSEAD, a business graduate school with locations in Europe, Asia, Middle East, and North America, I was fortunate to take the "Innovation Strategy and Entrepreneurship" class taught by Dr. Ron Adner. The unique class was sixteen sessions long, and fifteen of the sessions were devoted to case studies. Each case study was a deep dive into an exciting innovation that was about to change the world— and then, in the end, it didn't. Ron used each session to help us understand why failure happens.

The title of this book, *Anticipate Failure*, is inspired by the user name ("expect") and password ("failure") required to access the website where we could download class materials and where Ron set up a student discussion board. His teaching has been an indispensable toolkit for me through the years, and I am eternally grateful to him.

Many of the founders and others I've worked with have built amazing businesses, but I've also worked on many promising ideas with talented people that ended in failures. My goal in writing this book is to share what I've learned with people who are on their own entrepreneurial journey—to help and empower them to build great companies that have the potential to change the world.

For entrepreneurship and business building to thrive, there must be a high tolerance for failure. The ultimate goal, of course, is not to fail. But failure is something we should always expect and anticipate. If you fail—and you surely will—learn from it and move forward. Every successful endeavor that I've been part of has had a lot of little failures along the way. In my experience, the ventures that eventually succeed are those that realize when they are getting into little failure modes, understand where they are, and quickly turn these little failures around before they become big ones.

Instead of fearing failure, become acutely aware of what could cause failure in your business and industry, and build a toolkit for how to deal with it. This is how you will succeed eventually— and succeed *big*.

My intention is to give entrepreneurs the confidence they need to face the many difficult situations and failures they will encounter in their journey. They should not be afraid. Instead, they should feel empowered that they have a toolkit that's a way to look ahead, to see what might come, and to know that every success is built upon little failures that are overcome. You learn from the failures you overcome, and then build on them to create a successful venture.

As you soon will see, this is not a typical, prescriptive business book that tells you if you do these seven things or adopt these five habits, your success will be guaranteed. We've all read plenty of books that boil business success down to a set of simple things. But that's not how things work in the real world. The real world is much more complex, and it can't be encapsulated in a short prescription that applies in every circumstance, for every business or industry, or for every founder, executive, or leader.

In the pages that follow, I will provide the tools you need to turn failure into success. As you read the examples of failure in this book, please keep in mind that I am not asserting that there is only one reason for each of these failures. If I've learned anything in my many years working with startups, it's that there are often many causes behind any single failure, and nailing down the exact cause is like trying to nail down the exact reason for today's weather.

The focus of this book is therefore not on establishing scientific causality for business failure, but rather on helping you the practitioner recognize patterns of failure so you can better anticipate the possibilities for failure in your own organization. When failure arrives, which it inevitably will, you'll be better prepared to recognize and navigate your way through.

Failure is our constant companion and friend, there's no reason to fear it. Indeed, failure makes us better—it makes us stronger; it builds our resilience; it keeps us humble and hungry; and it provides the lessons we need to build growing businesses that create real value for customers, investors, and the communities in which they operate.

If you can achieve that, then you'll know real success.

CHAPTER ONE

FAILURE
IS COMMON

In an August 2018 press release, WndrCo Holdings announced that it had raised $1 billion in an initial funding round for its startup media platform, NewTV. According to the release, NewTV "brings together the best of Silicon Valley and Hollywood to create the first entertainment platform built for easy, on-the-go mobile viewing, allowing today's leading studios and creative talent to tell original stories in an entirely new way."[1]

The company took shape under the leadership of entertainment and tech dream duo Jeffrey Katzenberg and Meg Whitman, raised $1.75 billion, signed content from a deep bench of A-list celebrities, and presold much of its advertising inventory months before its launch. As Meg said in the early days of

NewTV, "It's a perfect marriage, in some ways, of Hollywood and Silicon Valley."[2] Just six months after it went live in April 2020, the company announced that it would shut down.

How could such a sure bet fail?

The idea was to deliver premium content—including star-studded original shows, news, lifestyle, and sports—directly to customers' phones. The content would be dispensed in "quick bites" of ten minutes or less, perfect for highly distractable consumers who rely on their smartphones to provide a steady stream of short-form videos (think TikTok), podcasts, Facebook feeds, news alerts, Instagram posts, music, games, apps, and more to entertain and inform them throughout the day. With an estimated 3.8 billion smartphone users worldwide, the potential market seemed enormous.[3]

While there are plenty of new media ventures in the works at any given time, several things separated NewTV from the rest of the pack. First, there was that $1 billion. Most of this small mountain of cash didn't come from the usual Silicon Valley venture capital firms. Instead, the majority was raised from a top-shelf list of Hollywood studios and media giants (Disney, Sony Pictures Entertainment, and Viacom), tech companies (Alibaba and Liberty Global), and investment banks (Goldman Sachs and JPMorgan Chase).[4]

Second, NewTV was helmed by two seasoned veterans of the entertainment and tech industries whose very presence assured many observers that the company was on the fast track to success. While the ultimate success of a new venture never can be guaranteed, Jeffrey Katzenberg and Meg Whitman had an enviable track record in their previous business leadership positions. They lent tremendous gravitas and credibility to the project.

Jeffrey is the longtime Hollywood insider who served as president of production for Paramount Studios, where he was involved in numerous popular films, including *Star Trek: The Motion Picture*, *Raiders of the Lost Ark*, and *Saturday Night Fever*. He became chairman of The Walt Disney Studios, helping revitalize Disney's animation business with *The Little Mermaid*, *Toy Story*, and *The Lion King* before leaving in 1994 to co-found his own highly successful film studios along with Stephen Spielberg and David Geffen. DreamWorks SKG and DreamWorks Animation were responsible for *The Prince of Egypt*, *Saving Private Ryan*, and *How to Train Your Dragon*.

He understood the people in the entertainment business, he had all the connections, and he was and still is deeply embedded in the industry. Because of his work in animation, he was also a pioneer at the intersection of technology and media. The film *Shrek*, which Jeffrey oversaw at DreamWorks Animation, was a milestone in the application of Hollywood cinematic techniques using advanced digital technology and animation. He grew DreamWorks into the largest animation studio in the world.

I had the good fortune to meet Jeffrey while I was at Hewlett-Packard because DreamWorks was one of HP's most important customers. He's the kind of entrepreneur that every investor wants to back—he's grounded in a wealth of experience, he's really well networked, he's got the gift to see the future and what it could bring, and he wins even when all the odds are stacked against him.

Meg Whitman served as CEO of eBay, taking the company from $5.7 million in sales in 1998 to $8 billion in sales by 2008. She told me the story of when eBay was trying to recruit her, and she went to meet with the founder, Pierre Omidyar. eBay was a ragtag operation at the time, and in order to make eBay look like a viable operation, the leadership team hired a reception-ist to sit at the front desk when they knew she was scheduled to arrive for her interview. They wanted Meg to believe she was dealing with a legitimate business and feel comfortable leaving behind her executive position with a well-established company. She was offered the job, and she accepted—staying for ten years. She joined eBay when it was a young company of about thirty people. When she left, it had grown to more than fifteen thousand employees.

A few years after she left eBay, Meg joined the HP board, then took over as CEO of Hewlett-Packard, and next as CEO of Hewlett Packard Enterprise. Today she sits on the boards of Procter & Gamble, General Motors, and Dropbox. I had a chance to work closely with her at HP, and I greatly admired her acumen and work ethic. Meg is the consummate Silicon Valley insider, widely networked and respected.

If you were to matchmake the perfect marriage of Silicon Valley and Hollywood, these are the two people you'd pick as partners. They are insiders steeped in their respective industries as well as knowledgeable about the other side. It also turns out that Jeffrey and Meg worked together at Disney a long, long time ago.

In addition to this leadership match made in heaven, the other thing working in NewTV's favor was that the timing seemed perfect to try this tech innovation. Smartphone screens were gaining in resolution and becoming more gorgeous with each new generation. Everybody had a smartphone, and people were shifting their time and attention from their televisions, desktop computers, and laptops to smartphones. Focusing product delivery on the smartphone seemed like a smart call.

Around that time, Netflix proved with its original series *House of Cards* that there would be a deeper collaboration between technology and content, and technology could provide digital distribution. It seemed that NewTV was the right idea at the right time with the right people.

By the end of 2018, NewTV had changed its name to Quibi—a short version of the "quick bites" of entertainment that Katzenberg envisioned, none longer than ten minutes. Each bite would be a complete story with a beginning, middle, and end—not just a film cut into fifteen ten-minute pieces.

In June 2019, Quibi announced the company had sold $100 million in advertising—representing two-thirds of the company's available advertising spots—well ahead of the planned 2020 launch.

In March 2020, one month before Quibi launched, the company announced that it had raised another $750 million for subscriber acquisition and that it had a stable of 50 shows ready for release, which would quickly grow to 175 shows.[5]

Quibi was launched with much fanfare in April 2020, just as the COVID-19 pandemic washed over the world, pushing an unprecedented number of people out of their workplaces, out of work, hunkered down in their homes, and looking for distractions from the increasingly grim reality of the pandemic. Seemingly it was the perfect time for a mobile-based entertainment venture to gain traction.

As it turned out, it wasn't—at least not for a platform filled with entertainment industry-generated content.

Despite the $1 billion in initial funding, the additional $750 million gathered along the way, the $100 million in ad sales, and the stellar creative and business management credentials of

Katzenberg and Whitman, in October 2020—six months after Quibi went live—the company announced that it would shut down before the end of the year.

What made Quibi swing from sure bet to business failure in little more than two years? How could such a promising idea with such an accomplished founding team, whose time had seemed to come, go so wrong so fast?

Actually it happens all the time.

SURE BETS AREN'T

The Tata Nano automobile was perfect for India, or so Tata Chairman Ratan Tata thought. The car—priced at 1 lakh rupees (about $2,500 at the time)—would provide a safe and affordable alternative to millions of customers who mostly used two-wheeled motor scooters to commute to work, go shopping, take their kids to school, and so on. Just ten years after introducing the car to the public with much fanfare, Tata pulled the plug on the apple of its chairman's eye. The Nano served a market need, and the base of potential customers was huge, but that turned out to be a mirage. Where did the customers go?

The Segway was a technological marvel that was touted to change urban transportation. Unfortunately for the company, it did not achieve that potential. These two-wheeled, self-balancing scooters didn't catch on for a variety of reasons, not the least of which was their high price. They became popular with just two groups of customers: tourists and mall cops. "Build it, and they will come" turned out to be a fallacy. Why did a world-changing technology not change the world?

British music conglomerate EMI used the royalties from The Beatles records it sold in the 1960s to help fund the development of the CT scanner—a device that fundamentally changed the practice of medicine worldwide. Although EMI invented CT technology, it was able to sell only a handful of the units, abandoning the market to Siemens and General Electric in 1976.[6] A common belief is that first movers win. But do they really? Why did second mover Siemens become the world's leading medical imaging company while first mover EMI failed to sustain its advantage?

When it was released to customers in 1993, the Apple Newton opened an entirely new product segment: the personal digital assistant (PDA), so named by Apple's then-CEO John Sculley. Combining email and fax capabilities, a calendar, a contacts directory, to-do lists, text input using a virtual keyboard, and more in a handheld device, there was every indication that the Newton quickly would become the preferred portable computing solution for millions of people. However, millions of people did *not* buy the Newton. In fact, while Apple sold fifty thousand of the devices in its first three months, sales quickly declined. Soon after Steve Jobs returned as Apple CEO in 1997, he killed the product. Was the Newton ahead of its time?

In September 2017, the first ten Bird dockless electric scooters were released onto the streets of Santa Monica, California, pioneering a seemingly unlimited micromobility market. Within a year, Bird sold more than ten million rides, established a presence in more than one hundred cities in the United States and around the globe, and was the startup to achieve a valuation of $2 billion the fastest.[7] Many more companies, including Lime, Spin, and Voi, quickly followed Bird's lead. Just when everyone believed that scooters would become ubiquitous, the tide began to turn. By 2020, in the wake of COVID-19 shutdowns, the number of global shared and private micromobility passenger-kilometers traveled declined by 60 to 70 percent, putting the market into a tailspin.[8] Why did electric scooters run out of juice?

Video surveillance cameras, building access controls, and other physical security systems are ubiquitous in both residential and commercial buildings today. While consumers embraced smart home products from companies such as Nest, Ring, and August, commercial customers suffered through antiquated, not-so-smart products. Many entrepreneurs tried to sell into the physical security market and failed due to entrenched incumbents, hard-to-penetrate channels, and commoditization by Chinese competitors such as Hikvision. The sure bet was to avoid the commercial physical security market, and it languished without meaningful innovation for decades. However, one company, Verkada, took on this space and emerged as an industry leader. What enabled Verkada to succeed where others failed, putting it on track to hypergrowth?

We are biased by big successes that seem like sure bets in hindsight, from electrical engineer/inventor Werner von Siemens to automobile industrialist Henry Ford, from Apple CEO Steve Jobs to Amazon CEO Jeff Bezos. The truth is that failure is more common in endeavors that look like sure bets at the beginning. About half of new businesses in the United States survive five years, while only a third make it to their tenth anniversary.[9] Even the ones that become sustainable and profitable in the long run experience many moments of failure that challenge their leadership teams, sometimes to the limit, before they are overcome. It is harder than ever to sustain success. The churn rate of companies in the S&P 500 is soon expected to hit 50 percent every decade.[10]

Sometimes we don't notice failure because of our predilection for success stories, falling victim to survivorship bias. Technology media, for example, celebrate the hugely successful startup founders, conferring them celebrity status on par with movie stars. Nobody writes about failures unless they are spectacular, as in the case of Theranos and its blood analyzer. The fact is that startup failures vastly outnumber the outlier successes.

Failures can happen for many reasons, but they should not be catastrophic. If we anticipate failure, we can take action to avoid or minimize the negative impacts so that we ultimately can succeed.

SEVEN PATTERNS OF FAILURE

There are many ways to fail in the innovation and entrepreneurial journey. Anticipating them, preparing relentlessly for them, and navigating through them when they do happen is the way to achieve success. In my many years observing the roots of failure of promising businesses run by talented people, I have found that seven patterns of failure tend to dominate. They are:

- Customer failure
- Technology failure
- Product failure
- Team failure
- Timing failure
- Business model failure
- Execution failure

In the chapters that follow, I will address each of these patterns, providing case studies and examples of companies that failed despite the best intentions and the many good things they had going for them. My goal is to sensitize you to failure to ensure that you know it is always right around the corner and you are ready to take it on. Remember: Companies often face some combination of these patterns of failure at the same time, not just one.

Instead of failing, you can quickly pivot your organization in response to a fast-changing business environment as Bizzabo did. Not familiar with Bizzabo? Let's talk about that company next.

TURNING POTENTIAL FAILURE TO BIG OPPORTUNITY

The meetings industry is *huge*—encompassing everything from offsite executive team gatherings, to conferences, shareholder meetings, trade shows, company-sponsored parties, product launch events, and much more. According to a 2018 study of the meetings industry sponsored by the Events Industry Council and conducted by Oxford Economics, nearly two million meetings took place in the United States in 2016. (For the purpose of the study, a meeting was defined as a gathering of ten or more participants for a minimum of four hours in a contracted venue.) The results indicated that such meetings involved about 250 million participants and generated $325 billion in direct spending, including expenditures to plan and produce the meetings, travel to and from the venues, and more.[11]

At least, this was the case before the COVID-19 pandemic brought most live events to a screeching halt, causing organizations to scramble for an alternative to in-person events.

While large companies often have in-house events teams embedded in their marketing or sales departments, many companies contract out their events to firms that specialize in making them happen. One such company is Bizzabo.

Bizzabo was founded in 2011 to help connect professional event attendees. After attending numerous events themselves, the three founders—Alon Alroy, Eran Ben-Shushan, and Boaz Katz—realized that the events industry desperately needed a major technology infusion. This sparked the idea for their startup. Said Eran, who serves as Bizzabo's CEO:

> We started Bizzabo because we realized that events were broken. Back then, events and technology were disconnected. Mobile, cloud, big data, and social networking were becoming mainstream, but events weren't taking advantage of these technologies—they were stuck in the past. So you would go to an event, and you would ask, "Wait, I have LinkedIn on my mobile phone and can do all sorts of things with it. How come I cannot be much more efficient in networking or consuming content and knowing how to manage my time at this event?" That's how we started our journey.

They initially built their business using friends and family investments, with each of the three principals taking a different role. Alon focused on business development and marketing, Boaz on product and technology, and Eran on business operations and management. The company's initial product was a mobile app for connecting event attendees. All was going well with their initial product until the founders realized after a couple of years that the scope of their product and their vision were not big enough. This was their "Houston, we have a problem" moment.

Bizzabo was well funded, was selected as one of the best startups in Israel, and was gaining traction with its product. But the writing was on the wall: The product was never going to be a mission-critical platform that the company could build a sustainable business around. This led to Bizzabo's first pivot. According to Eran:

> *We understood that our product was not going to fly, but we also knew what was missing because our customers told us. They kept telling us, "You built a great product, but can you build around it all the other tools that we need in order to run events—the website, the registration, the scheduling, and all the rest?" We knew that if we didn't respond to what our customers actually needed, we were going to fail. So we went to the board, we went to our wives, we went to our employees, and we said, "We know we sold you very heavily over the last two and a half years that this is going to be a rocket ship. We now realize that it's not the case. But we know what we need to do." We had to get buy-in by everyone, and we did. Everyone bought into the idea, and we had our first very successful pivot.*

This was a big bet for Bizzabo, but it was a necessary one. The events platform that customers wanted did not exist in the market, so Bizzabo committed to designing and building it. It took about a year for the company to integrate its new product vision into the existing platform, and this effort was instrumental to Bizzabo's continued success. The company's event management platform grew to provide client companies with the ability to build websites around their events, manage event registration, sell tickets, integrate mobile, track return on investment (ROI), manage speakers and agendas, and grow communities.

Said Eran, "When we launched our new platform into the market, it started smelling like we hit something big—we had product-market fit." With its new product in hand, Bizzabo signed deals with an impressive roster of clients, including Uber, Inbound, Rakuten, Gainsight, and Accenture.

This led to Bizzabo's next challenge: scaling the team and the go-to-market functions while building a culture that remained loyal to its startup days. This was Bizzabo's second successful pivot, although it presented its own set of challenges to be overcome. Said Eran about that time:

> We made a lot of mistakes, a lot of bad hires, but we also got some things right. And we evolved—we constantly evolve. We realized that we were going to be a SaaS company. And the lifetime value of our customers is top of mind for us, which helped us define the focus in the market. We started going more upmarket—first to mid-market and then to enterprise organizations.

In 2017, Bizzabo raised $15 million in a Series C round of equity funding, and in 2019, $27 million more in a Series D round of funding.[12] The company continued to grow, primarily focused on supporting live, in-person events. However, the COVID-19 pandemic changed everything for Bizzabo and the industry as a whole.

Literally overnight, organizations around the world canceled conferences, workshops, meetings, and all sorts of other in-person events. This sent event-planning companies scrambling to make up for the sudden change in their business environment.

Many events ended up moving online, often cobbled together by the organizations themselves. In one example, Web Summit, the largest European tech conference, had to move its 2020 conference from Lisbon to the online platform it built itself. More than one hundred thousand people from one hundred sixty-eight countries participated *remotely*.

What was a company that specialized in helping clients with in-person events to do when in-person events suddenly became outright ghosts?

In the case of Bizzabo, you don't sit on the sidelines and watch your revenue dry up and your business fail. You look for opportunities. This led to the company's third and most recent pivot. Bizzabo and similar companies were 100 percent focused on providing support for live, in-person events. While there were webinars and virtual meetings, full-scale virtual events didn't exist before COVID—there was no need for them. When meeting planners canceled thousands of events in the wake of the global pandemic, this left Bizzabo and its competitors scrambling to respond.

In Bizzabo's case, the loss of events led the company to lay off 25 percent of its workforce. However, it also led to the creation of a completely virtual events platform that would support customers in the new COVID world. According to Eran, this capability led to a large surge in business for the company in 2020:

Our platform has seen unprecedented demand this year. Compared to the year prior, the number of events organized through us has grown 65 percent. Additionally, the number of attendees registering for events with Bizzabo has grown 500 percent, while overall usage is up 150x. With a vaccine likely and more hybrid events in the future, we anticipate even greater growth.[13]

Bizzabo has turned the corner, not only surviving but also thriving in a very different business landscape. Investors seem to agree. In December 2020, the company announced that it raised $138 million in a Series E round of funding. I imagine that when live events return in a post-COVID world, Bizzabo will be particularly well positioned to take advantage of the pent-up demand for businesspeople around the globe to reconnect in person once again—happily leaving behind their home offices, their dogs and cats, and their Zoom meetings. Since Bizzabo mastered the art of supporting virtual and hybrid meetings during the pandemic, the founders have all the bases covered.

By anticipating failure, you can do something about it when it knocks on your door. Instead of being caught flat-footed, you will be ready to take action when others are still wondering what happened. Even when things are not under your control, when unanticipated events and challenges to your business hit you relentlessly and from every direction, you can *take* control.

Albert Einstein is often credited with saying, "In the midst of every crisis lies great opportunity." I believe those words. Adversity brings opportunity along with it. When you have a prepared mind, you will find ways to turn failure into success—moves you can make, levers you can pull, experiments you can try, lessons you can learn, and knowledge you can gain.

Anticipate failure and beat it on your journey to building a great business.

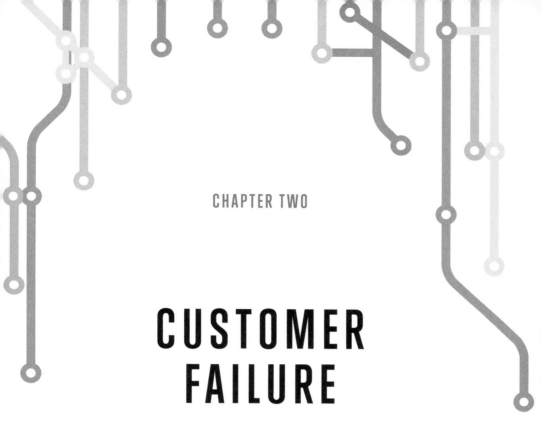

CHAPTER TWO

CUSTOMER FAILURE

Imagine that you had an idea for a $2,500 product with the strong potential to turn a significant portion of the fast-growing middle class of your country into customers. Sounds pretty good, right? Now imagine that the country we're talking about is India, and the potential market we're talking about numbers *three hundred million* people.

Now let's take this tremendous opportunity one step further. If the product succeeds in India, then there's every reason to believe that it would do just as well in other countries, adding potentially *billions* of customers to the mix.

This was the vision of Tata Group Chairman Ratan Tata, who envisioned the creation of a small, affordable "people's car" known as the Nano that would appeal directly to a large segment of India's population—the *three hundred million* customers mentioned.

However, when Tata pulled the plug on the car eleven years after it was unveiled to the public, it had sold a fraction of that, just three hundred thousand units, with 70 percent of those sold within the first four years.[14]

Where did all those customers go?

THE CHAIRMAN'S VISION

The Nano was first unveiled to the public in 2008—the brainchild of Ratan Tata, who was moved to action by an accident he observed six years earlier while driving on a busy city street on a rainy day. According to Tata, the idea for the Nano was sparked "when I observed families riding on two-wheelers, the father driving a scooter, his young kid standing in front of him, his wife sitting behind him holding a baby."[15]

As one of these two-wheelers with a family of four riding on it crossed an intersection just ahead of Tata's car, its tires slipped on the wet pavement, and the vehicle crashed to the ground. Although the family members weren't seriously injured, they certainly could have been. Tata recalled, "If we had been going faster, there would have been no way to keep from running over them. The family was all over the road and could have been under the car. I thought, *This is really bad*."[16]

Inspired by the accident, "I asked myself whether one could conceive of a safe, affordable, all-weather form of transport for such a family."[17]

Bengaluru, where Ratan Tata witnessed the two-wheeler accident, is subject to two different monsoon seasons, and urban floods often occur from August through October every year.[18] As you can imagine, people who rely on two-wheelers for transportation suffer when it rains. Riding is not only dirty, wet, and uncomfortable, but also dangerous. Road accidents in India involving two-wheelers result in approximately forty-seven thousand deaths each year. With approximately 1 percent of the entire vehicle population worldwide, India experiences 6 percent of traffic accidents globally.[19]

Despite the fact that India has one of the fastest-growing economies in the world, many of its citizens have been left behind. According to the World Bank, a little more than 43 percent of Indians—about 580 million people—are at or below the lower-middle-income class poverty line of $3.20 a day. About 139 million (10.4 percent) of Indians have incomes at or below the international poverty line of $1.90 a day.[20] In addition, those Indians in rural areas tend to experience greater levels of poverty than those in urban areas.

The hope was that at a price of 1 lakh rupees (about $2,500 at the time[21])—for the base, no-frills model—would enable a significant number of people to trade in their uncomfortable and unsafe motor scooters for the more comfortable and safer Nano.

Kevin and Jackie Freiberg wrote the best-selling book *Nuts! Southwest Airlines' Crazy Recipe for Business and Personal Success*. The book documented how then-Southwest Airlines chairman, CEO, and co-founder Herb Kelleher democratized the skies by building a safe, affordable, low-cost airline with a great employee culture. When the Freibergs approached Tata to write a book about the Nano (*Nanovation: How a Little Car Can Teach the World to Think Big and Act Bold*), they saw echoes of the Southwest Airlines story. As Kevin told me:

> *What attracted us to the Nano story was that Herb Kelleher wanted to democratize the American skies, and here Ratan Tata wanted to democratize the Indian roads. If there was a way to help people get a safe and affordable form of transportation from the villages into the cities where there were jobs, health care, education, and other opportunities—elevating the bottom of the pyramid—that would be a very noble, a very heroic journey. We wanted to be a part of telling that story.*

The Tata Nano had everything going for it—the personal support and vision of the powerful chairman of one of India's largest companies, the tried-and-true automotive technology that had been honed for more than a century, an inspiring social mission, and an untapped market of many millions of people. Yet the business failed.

Which brings us to the question: Why?

The key reason behind the Nano's failure was that Tata Motors did not fully understand the needs of the customers it had targeted. The company did not anticipate customer failure, and that doomed the Nano even before its tires hit the road for the very first time.

The idea of every new business is built on a hypothesis about a customer problem, and then a hypothesis about what product or service you will offer to solve that problem, which I address in Chapter 4, "Product Failure." In order to make it a business, you need a third component, which is a business model or a profitable transaction for the person who is actually solving the problem. I address this third component in Chapter 7, "Business Model Failure." When you start a business, you need to have a hypothesis for all of these different pieces.

From a customer perspective, as you're thinking about it, these three things come together between the builder of the business and the customer to create a profitable, enduring business with value on both sides. That's the economic theory behind this process. Nano started with a customer hypothesis.

A customer hypothesis (the *needs* hypothesis or the *problem* hypothesis) is that there are many people in India, particularly in urban areas, who rely on motorcycles and mopeds for transportation. In addition, a significant number are making the transition from the working class to the middle class. They have needs for commuting and for family transportation—taking their kids to school or sports activities. However, they can't afford an entry-level car because their income doesn't support such an expense. In other words, the price of the entry-level car was a singular barrier.

It was in one such city, Bengaluru, where Ratan Tata observed the family riding their two-wheeler in the rain and where he first formed his customer hypothesis. He thought, "Look, there's a customer problem. As people are moving up from the lower class to the middle class, they need a solution for their transportation needs. Let's provide it to them."

On the product side, Tata's hypothesis for the product that would solve the customer problem was as follows: "A two-wheeler is inherently unstable, and it doesn't provide protection for passengers in the event of bad weather or an accident. We have the ability to build a four-wheeled vehicle that can fit a family of four, so instead of being drenched in the rain on a two-wheeler, they can be stable and safe and protected in a four-wheeler. And as a car, it doesn't just meet their transportation needs, but also their aspirational needs."

Finally, the hypothesis for the business model was, "The person we're targeting cannot afford even the entry-level car, so we have to make a stripped-down car that is only slightly more expensive than a two-wheeler. At this entry point, we can sell this car to these people for 1 lakh rupees and still make some money. If you take a country of a billion people, at least a third of them were aspiring to move to the middle class and therefore could be the addressable market for this product."

These were the three key hypotheses that drove the development of Nano. Unfortunately, by following the very top-down hypothesis of Tata's chairman, the company missed the entire step in the middle—testing the hypotheses by actually talking with the customers and deeply understanding what their real needs were and what real problems needed solving. Tata's managers were convinced they had a viable business idea, and so they designed the car, did the trade-offs, built the factory, and started marketing Nano heavily. They jumped immediately from Ratan Tata's vision to execution of the product.

As it turned out, this was a mistake.

THE PROBLEM HYPOTHESIS VS. THE CUSTOMER HYPOTHESIS

If you're serious about business building, then you need to anticipate failure and avoid it. This means that you must test the *problem* hypothesis before you test the *solution* hypothesis.

The question that must be asked is, "Is this a real problem, and who is this a problem for?" For example, is daily commuting a problem for the group of people that we expect to become our customers? In the case of many Indian city dwellers, yes, it is a problem. But this problem is already solved adequately by existing solutions: public transportation, motorized two-wheelers, bicycles, or simply walking to work, the market, a child's school, or wherever else they need to go.

There's another part of the customer hypothesis to consider: Does the customer view this as a problem for them to take on the added expense of buying a car? For example, will the number of days in the year when they might have to drive in the rain compel them to change the transportation mode they have today? Would the improved safety or perceived upgrade in social status be enough?

Said Kevin Freiberg:

> *I think what they missed was the customer cultural aspect of this project. They were so focused on engineering—can we build a car that will sell to the public for 1 lakh rupees? Can we build a car that gets 50+ miles to the gallon? Can it be safe? Can it be somewhat attractive? Those were all product engineering innovation questions, and they had lots of starts and restarts in that process. Make no mistake about it, there were customers interested in buying the car—I believe they had one hundred thousand preorders secured. But those orders were not from the bottom of the pyramid. I believe the majority of those first cars were initially ordered by the wealthy as toys or to give to their driver, butler, or maid, so the help wouldn't come to work sweaty and dirty. This defeated the noble purpose of Nano.*

Freiberg also pointed out that Tata managers didn't have their eye on the ball when it came to building a car targeted to low-income people who aspire to rise into the middle class. The company didn't consider the question of where customers are in their financial journeys. Many of these customers didn't have bank accounts, and they didn't know how to talk to a banker about securing an auto loan—it was scary to them. For those who had enough money tucked under their mattress to afford to buy the car, there was the question of how to pay for ongoing maintenance and service.

Finally, Tata didn't realize that a cheap car could be perceived by the public as just that: a cheap car for poor people, not an aspirational car for those rising to the middle class. There was a stigma attached to the car. No one wanted to be seen as part of the bottom of the pyramid. No one wanted to tell the world that they had bought a cheap car because that was all they could afford.

If Tata staffers had spoken with more real customers, they would have found that their target demographic first of all cares a lot about their children's education. They care a lot about taking care of their older parents. They care a lot about buying a house. Buying a car is farther down the wish list. People in this segment have many other things they want to buy before they start thinking about solving their transportation problem with a luxury item. To truly understand these concerns, you have to put yourself in your customer's shoes.

Then there are middle-class people who might be thinking about buying a car. For them, the idea is to signal a change in social status, and buying a cheap car doesn't accomplish that. For them, neither the cost nor a transportation problem is the biggest issue. Signaling the status change is at the top of the list.

At the outset, you think you have a tremendous opportunity—*three hundred* million potential customers. Eventually you discover that because of the way you characterized the problem, you don't have that many customers. You've constrained your universe of buyers.

The right thing to do when you reach that point is to dig in, study the problem, and talk to your potential customers. You've decided that your product solves a variety of problems for them, but does it cause any new problems? Talk to people in the city who barely have space to park their two-wheelers. Your product is larger than a two-wheeler, which poses a new problem of parking it. Some of your target customers live in areas where there's petty crime, and now they have to worry about thieves breaking their windows, vandals scratching their paint, or others stealing their wheels and tires.

If Tata managers had tested their hypotheses up front with more real customers, they might have a better grasp of the issues. While customers wanted the Nano, and it solved part of their problems (for example, keeping the rain off their heads), it also created new problems (for example, finding parking).

The fact that Tata didn't fully understand the Nano's customers is particularly surprising considering that the company did extensive research with customers when it developed the Ace minitruck, which was released in 2005. In that case, Tata totally nailed the customer and created a huge hit—selling more than two million units within twelve years after its introduction.[22] Kevin and Jackie Freiberg described how Girish Wagh, the Ace project manager, approached his market research:

Girish and his fellow team members went out to see what people needed. And our wording is very exact: They didn't go to find out what people thought of them or their products, and they didn't hold focus groups to see if people liked their ideas. They went to see what people needed. They went to the bazaars and the small factories. They went to the villages. They talked to farmers, truckers, builders, and small entrepreneurs. They asked endless questions, and they listened to the answers.[23]

Now, back to the Nano. Tata was able to build and deliver the product, but not without making some serious compromises. Developing a car to sell at such a low price point meant cutting a lot of corners. Steering was manual, and the base model had no air conditioning. Parts were glued instead of welded together, tires were just twelve inches in diameter, and there were no airbags.[24] Higher-level models of the Nano offered upgrades such as air conditioning, but the base 1 lakh rupees model was as bare-bones as it could be.

Then there was the issue of safety or lack thereof. The nonprofit Global New Car Assessment Programme (Global NCAP) awarded the Nano *zero* stars in its frontal impact crash test at sixty-four kilometers an hour, stating that "the vehicle structure proved inadequate and collapsed to varying degrees, resulting in high risks of life-threatening injuries to the occupants."[25] In addition, reports and photos of Nanos that spontaneously caught fire became common in the press and social media.

The base model turned out to cost more to build than the 1 lakh rupees it initially sold for. As a letter sent to the directors of Tata Sons by former Chairman Cyrus Mistry shortly after he was dismissed from the company explained:

The Nano product development concept called for a car below Rs 1 lakh, but the costs were always above this. This product has consistently lost money, peaking at Rs 1000 crores. As there is no line of sight to profitability for the Nano, any turnaround strategy for the company requires to shut it down. Emotional reasons alone have kept us away from this crucial decision.[26]

Clearly, while Tata was able to build and market the car, the customer side was where everything began to fall apart. Further, Tata could not deliver on the promised customer value proposition: A quality product that was safe, easy to use, and easy to service.

If you unwind the customer failure part of the Tata Nano now and consider what things you can take out of it, I think you could say, "Every business starts with this component of what is the problem, what is the solution, and why is it a compelling business?"

It's great to start with a hypothesis, and sometimes these hypotheses look fantastic. The real test comes when you have to go through the verification phase. You can't go directly into implementation because the verification phase makes sure that the pain point is compelling, and the customer indeed has a pain point. Usually, a good indication that it's an important thing to them is that customers are thinking about it every day, using some other approach to solving the problem, and incurring costs today because of the problem. When they hear about the product and its features, they believe it's a great fit that meets their need, and they would be willing to pay for it.

This all adds up to having a hypothesis with a customer, testing it early with many customers, and understanding who the customers are. Do they have a pain point, and are there enough who will pay for it? Understanding the customer pain point also means asking, "Are there any significant barriers to adoption?" (such as not having a parking place for their new Nanos). Avoid falling too much in love with the product and the way you conceived it, and really do proper customer discovery. Speak to a variety of customers in depth—walking a mile in their shoes and not having just a couple of superficial conversations that confirm your hypothesis.

Those are the kinds of things that can help you avoid customer failure. When in doubt, verify and iterate. Don't be so stuck to your hypothesis that you ignore any evidence that shows it's wrong or needs revision. It's much easier to correct course in this phase before you commit to building a specific product or to adopting a specific business model and realize that you've got one of these things wrong.

In the startup world, we speak to entrepreneurs every day who have a product idea and have spoken to a few customers in their network who seem to be interested. We then ask: "Is it a vitamin or a painkiller for the customer?" If you are in pain, you clearly have a problem that needs to be solved. There's a compelling reason for you to solve it, and if a painkiller is proven to be effective, you're going to pay for it and take it.

Vitamins are different—they are optional. Sure, the supplement industry is large, but if you're selling a vitamin, maybe people will buy it, and maybe they won't. Customers don't need to make a decision right away as there is no pain today, and they are not very loyal. If they stop taking the vitamin, it doesn't really change their life.

LESSONS FROM NANO

When we scrutinize the failure of the Nano, we can see a variety of potential points of customer failure when creating and selling a new product or service. It's your job to anticipate and avoid them at the inception of a new business.

- When a product is conceived and built first as a technological marvel. Only then does the business begin its search for customers. Creating a real automobile priced at just 1 lakh rupees was quite an accomplishment, but it was driven by a perceived need based on an anecdote.

- When a customer need is perceived, but it is not actually real and not thoroughly vetted through customer conversations. Tata did not do a proper job talking with potential customers to find out what they really wanted and needed, and why.

- When there is a real customer need, but the pain is not high enough for all the targeted customers to pay for it. People may show initial interest, but that does not translate to the majority of them opening their wallets. While about one hundred thousand people put down deposits to purchase the car before it was available for sale, only three hundred thousand Nanos were sold during the course of its production—most within the first three or four years after the car became available for purchase.[27]

- When customers are willing to pay for a new solution, but the benefits of the offered solution do not outweigh the switching cost of an existing, imperfect solution. In reality, the Nano created an entirely new set of problems for customers, such as how they would finance the vehicle, where they would park it, and so on.

- When the segment of customers who are willing to pay is really small, and the solution is not applicable beyond the segment.
- When early adopters in a market segment are willing to experiment with the new product, but the majority of the market is not accessible or available for any of the preceding reasons.

COACHING THROUGH CUSTOMER FAILURE

The good news is that you don't have to fail when it comes to your customers. There are a variety of things you can and should do to anticipate customer failure and ensure it doesn't impede your success. Start with a hypothesis for your business. The hypothesis is usually, "There's a customer problem, and there's a product that solves that problem." Next you'll create a business model to serve the customers you identify, but you must be careful not to step directly into execution. Verify and test each one of your hypotheses and iterate through them. Your goal is to fully understand:

- Is this a real problem?
- Is the problem threshold high enough that your target customers are really seeking a solution, or is it a minor inconvenience that they would be willing to live with forever?
- Are there enough customers with this problem?
- Is this a repeatable problem?
- What customer segments exist that have the problem?
- What other options exist to solve the problem?

Aiming broadly and saying, "Half the people in India have this problem," for example, as Tata did with the Nano, seldom works.

It is not uncommon for entrepreneurs to start their pitch to me saying, "According to [their favorite market research firm], this is a $100 billion market, and every business in the world is a potential customer." You have to start with a much smaller target surface of people who have the problem as you focus and hone the early testing of your hypothesis. Don't lose sight of that broader customer group, however, because those are the people you can sell your product to later.

Really get down to it in characterizing the problem, verifying it, and making sure it fits with your hypotheses. If it doesn't fit, iterate. Always think in terms of: *What is your offer? Is this the product offer that hits the bull's-eye and perfectly solves the customer's problem?* If it doesn't, then try again.

Consider whether the product you're going to offer is a painkiller or a vitamin. Is the pain high enough that customers actually will pay to buy this product or only will pay lip service? A vitamin is a convenience, and when push comes to shove, will they decline to pay for it? With respect to the product, are you creating other inconveniences because of it? Are there side effects or unintended consequences from buying the product that will hinder a good fit for customers? Will they be willing to switch from what they're using now—something that doesn't solve the pain, but is familiar—and adopt your new offering?

You will need to test all of these hypotheses so that if there's failure in any one of them, you can go back and iterate. By doing so, you can avoid customer failure. Once you settle on your hypotheses and take the time to test them, you will save a tremendous amount of time, money, and failures down the line. For example, when you hire two hundred people to sell to your target customers, but completely change direction when you suddenly discover that customers won't buy it, that will be extremely expensive compared with getting the customer right from the outset.

Steve Blank was one of the first to create a framework and coach entrepreneurs specifically on how to avoid customer failure. Let's pause to delve deeper into Steve's coaching, which I have found valuable. In his book *The Four Steps to the Epiphany*, Steve writes: "Startups don't fail because they lack a product; they fail because they lack customers and a proven financial model."[28] I was fortunate to meet him early in my venture career when the firm I worked for invested in IMVU, a networking site where he served on the board. The company's founder, Eric Ries, later wrote *The Lean Startup*, inspired in great part by Steve's foundational thinking around customers.

In his book, Steve explains the Product Development model that has dominated business for the past century. In the first step of this model, *Concept*, "Founders capture their passion and vision for the company and turn them into a set of key ideas, which quickly becomes a business plan."[29] The second step, *Development*, centers around defining exactly what the new product or service will be, what its anticipated features and benefits are, and whether it is technically feasible. The third step, *Testing*, is where customers finally enter the picture. Who are they, and where can we find them? Finally, in the fourth step,

Figure 2-1: The Product Development Model

Launch, we consider distribution, competition, positioning in the marketplace, and pricing.

According to Steve, this approach is all wrong. In fact, in his book, he points out major flaws for using the Product Development model to launch a new product. These flaws include failing to focus on developing customers and markets, giving learning and discovery short shrift in favor of execution, premature scaling, and more.

A much better approach, Steve says, is what he calls the Customer Development model, which properly puts the emphasis on the *customer*—discovering markets, finding the first customers, validating assumptions, and growing the business. his Customer Development model has just four steps:

- **Customer Discovery.** In this step, you determine who the customers are for your new product and whether the problem you are trying to solve with it is actually important to them.
- **Customer Validation.** In this step, you prove that you have located customers who will buy your product and that a market exists. The goal of this step is to create a sales road map—a field-tested sales process playbook.
- **Customer Creation.** In this step, you build on your initial sales, creating end-user demand and then driving that demand into your company's sales channel. How you approach this step will depend on the nature of company and product—for example, bringing a new product into a new market versus an existing market.
- **Company Building.** In the final step, you move the new product "from an informal, learning and discovery-oriented Customer Development team into

formal departments," such as Sales, Marketing, and Business Development. One thing to watch out for is premature scaling, where a company spends heavily on a new product and supporting infrastructure without first going through a rigorous process of Customer Discovery and Validation.

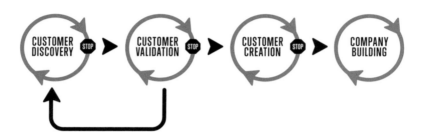

Figure 2-2: The Customer Development Model

Steve cautions that the Customer Development model is not a replacement for the Product Development model—*that* model is still a necessary part of building and launching great products. Instead, the Customer Development model and the Product Development model will ideally be used together—each providing a necessary part of the puzzle.

We start with customer failure in this book because customers are the raison d'être for a business. Understanding, serving, and delighting customers never goes out of fashion, no matter what stage a business is in. For a new business, getting customers right and avoiding customer failure is an existential priority.

CHAPTER THREE

TECHNOLOGY FAILURE

The Segway PT (Personal Transporter) was a marvel of technology: a two-wheeled, stand-up, single-rider electric scooter with a maximum range of twelve miles on a single charge at speeds up to twelve and a half miles per hour.[30] Introduced to the public in 2001 on ABC television's popular *Good Morning America* show, the product quickly captured the interest of the American public.

And what a product it was. The machine—invented by Dean Kamen, who holds more than a thousand patents[31]—was made up of an innovative network of five gyroscopic and two acceleration sensors with the ability to analyze the environment and the rider's position one hundred times per second, as well as a drive system, a steering system, and several breakthroughs in robotics engineering.

The Segway PT's advanced technology came at a price: $4,950, or about one-third the price of a new entry-level Honda Accord at the time.[32]

Kamen billed the Segway PT as a replacement for automobiles, saying it "will be to the car what the car was to the horse and buggy." In 2002, Tobe Cohen, Segway's director of marketing and brand strategy, projected that the company would sell up to one hundred thousand units a year beginning in 2003. John Doerr predicted that Segway would hit $1 billion in sales faster than any company ever and that the company might turn out to be "bigger than the Internet itself."[33]

In short, the Segway PT was poised to transform transportation as we knew it. That is, until it wasn't. The hype cycle soon wore off, and the reality of market adoption set in. The company struggled for many years to sell enough units to build a sustainable business. Segway finally pulled the plug on its electric standup scooter in 2020, five years after the company was acquired by Ninebot, a Chinese company that specialized in building inexpensive consumer-grade electric kick scooters. The grand total number of Segways sold? About 140,000.[34] Why didn't Segway's remarkable technology make it the winner it was predicted to be?

A TALE OF TWO COMPANIES

When the Segway was introduced to the world in 2001, inventor Dean Kamen made a promise: that his invention—a stand-up, electric scooter for one—would forever transform urban transportation. At the time, urban transportation was well established and well defined. There were aircraft, trains, subways, and automobiles; motorcycles and scooters; taxis and rental cars; and bicycles and skateboards for the more intrepid.

However, after inventing the iBOT—an electric wheelchair that had the unique ability to climb stairs, navigate a variety of terrains both indoors and outside, and enable the rider to stand at full height—Kamen set his sights on creating a new form of mobility that would revolutionize the way we travel. His invention would provide customers with a fast, convenient, and inexpensive way to go to work, go shopping, and take on other day-to-day local tasks while forgoing automobiles and other traditional forms of transportation. He code named his invention "Ginger," called it the Segway HT (Human Transporter) when first introduced, and eventually christened it Segway PT (Personal Transporter) on commercial launch.

To say that his product was a tremendous technological achievement would be an understatement. The Segway PT was the world's first self-balancing, stand-up electric scooter. There was nothing like it before its introduction and for years after. The machine itself was an innovative collection of sensors, gyroscopes, computer hardware and software, electric motors, and a large nickel metal-hydride battery. According to a 2001 *Time* magazine article:

> *Developed at a cost of more than $100 million, Kamen's vehicle is a complex bundle of hardware and software that mimics the human body's ability to maintain its balance. Not only does it have no brakes; it also has no engine, no throttle, no gearshift, and no steering wheel. And it can carry the average rider for a full day, nonstop, on only five cents' worth of electricity.*[35]

As opposed to riding a bike, you could just stand on it, and it would take you safely from Place A to Place B. The amount of technology that went into the Segway—the gyroscopic sensors, the onboard computer and software doing all the calculations to turn left or right, go backward or forward, or spin in place while constantly balancing the weight of the scooter and rider was truly remarkable. The Segway was way ahead of its time in terms of the mechanical and electrical engineering involved and the computer hardware and software all working together seamlessly.

When he introduced the Segway to the public on *Good Morning America*, Kamen described the technology that made his invention work in very human terms:

> *It does what a human does. It has gyros and sensors that act like your inner ear. It has a computer that does what your brain does for you. It's got motors that do what your muscles do for you. It's got those tires that do what your feet do for you.*[36]

Creating all this remarkable technology was just the beginning. Once the product was developed, then there had to be a vision in place for what to do with it. Fortunately, when it came to its inventor, there was no lack of a vision. Kamen didn't envision that the Segway PT would entirely replace cars, trucks, trains, buses, or other long-distance forms of transportation. Instead, he was focused on shorter distances, particularly the so-called "last mile" connecting people who arrive in urban environments on public transportation to their offices and other destinations.

Said Kamen: "Cars are great for going long distances, but it makes no sense at all for people in cities to use a 4,000-pound piece of metal to haul their 150-pound asses around town." Further, "If we're successful, if enough of these become part of the infrastructure, what will happen is people will start to take back the very core of their cities." Jeff Bezos called it "one of the most famous and anticipated product introductions of all time."[37] Even Steve Jobs bought into Kamen's vision. Said Jobs: "If enough people see this machine, you won't have to convince them to architect cities around it; it'll just happen."[38]

Getting large numbers of people out of their cars and onto rechargeable electric vehicles would indeed be a major transformation of the transportation sector. However, as Kamen learned, it would take more than remarkable technology to turn his vision into reality.

Yes, Segway's technology was amazing, but...

At a retail price of just under $5,000, the Segway became a toy for well-heeled buyers, not ordinary consumers who either could not afford it or were afraid they would be making a life-and-death financial decision by buying one.

Beyond the high price of admission, the world was not yet ready to buy an electric vehicle—especially an electric vehicle with a range of just twelve miles on a good day and no protection of riders from the rain, wind, cold, and other elements.

The Segway PT lacked the infrastructure needed to truly transform transportation. The owners were pioneers who had to figure out where they could ride their vehicles, where they could recharge them, where they could park them, and so on.

Learning how to operate the scooter was a headache. Riding a Segway PT was different from riding a bicycle or motorcycle, requiring an entirely new set of skills. The first customers had to travel to regional training centers for lessons.

There was an element of risk to riders. President George W. Bush was photographed falling off a Segway while on vacation in Maine; television personality Piers Morgan fell off a Segway and broke three ribs; and the onetime owner of the Segway company, James Heselden, was killed when he accidentally ran his Segway off a cliff. The press was full of reports of Segway accidents, some leaving riders seriously injured.

A lot of pedestrians didn't want to share sidewalks with them. Segways moved quickly and quietly, surprising pedestrians when the vehicles approached from behind. Unlike the ride-hailing and scooter startups of today, Segway spent years working within the federal, state, and local government systems to win friends and change rules with patchy results.

Then there was the nerd factor. When Segways started showing up on city streets, it was clear to most that early adopters were tech-savvy people with more disposable income than they knew what to do with. According to a CNN article, "it was hard to look like anything other than a nerd riding one. It became a punchline, and then a trope, as a prop in television shows like *Arrested Development* and movies like *Mall Cop*."

There were problems with the product itself, too. In 2006, the U.S. Consumer Product Safety Commission issued a voluntary recall of Segway scooters due to a software glitch that could "unexpectedly apply reverse torque to the wheels." In other words, suddenly put the scooter into reverse while it was moving forward. According to Segway at the time, the problem had resulted in six head and wrist injuries.[39]

The recall also revealed an uncomfortable truth about Segway: The company had sold only 23,500 Segways from the product's introduction through mid-2006, or fewer than 5,000 a year. This was a tiny fraction of the 100,000 units a year projected by Tobe Cohen, the company's director of marketing and brand strategy. According to one article published at the time, "Five years after its launch, the Segway is what it always was and may always be: an overhyped disappointment."[40]

All these things and more led to the failure of Segway and its stand-up scooters. The company was sold off to Ninebot, a Chinese electric kick scooter manufacturer, in 2015. Ninebot became phenomenally successful when Bird made scooter-sharing a thing in 2017, putting Ninebot in position to sell millions of its electric kick scooters. They cost a fraction of the price of a Segway, they were easy to use and maintain, and they had the *cool* factor at the time that Segway never had. We'll dig deeper into that story in Chapter 7, "Business Model Failure."

What about the company that eventually did change urban mobility, Uber? When Uber (originally called Ubercab) was founded in 2009, the idea was to take the pain out of hailing a taxicab in a busy city. In his investment memo on Uber, Sequoia scout Jason Calacanis wrote just two words, speaking directly to this pain point: "Cabs suck."[41]

Using a simple phone app, with a few clicks you could request a black limo car service to pick you up on demand—whenever you wanted and wherever you might be—and deliver you to your destination. While technology was involved, there was nothing particularly remarkable about it. Uber ran on a smartphone app that used ubiquitous 3G wireless mobile telecommunications technology, Google Maps, and GPS location systems to track the location of customers and drivers (already built into smartphones), and a lot of cloud computing, which was provided by Amazon Web Services (AWS). The only other thing needed was a network of drivers, most using their own cars.

Uber sparked an entirely new industry, ride-sharing, and it quickly gained popularity. In 2014, Uber delivered one hundred forty million trips, and just five years later this number exploded to nearly seven billion trips a year.[42] As its popularity grew, Uber quickly broadened its driver network to include all sorts of cars, not just black limos. Soon it seemed as if every other Toyota Prius driving the streets of major cities had an Uber sticker in its window. As of December 2020, the company delivers sixteen million trips a day, in almost ten thousand cities in seventy-one countries around the world.[43]

While Dean Kamen's vision was to transform transportation, the Segway failed to achieve that goal despite its remarkable technology. When Uber was conceived, the founders did not have deep technology and weren't looking to transform transportation: They just wanted to provide users with a more reliable way of quickly summoning a ride when taxicabs were hard to get.

As you have gathered by now, when we talk about technology failure, we are not focused on what innards the invention has and whether it actually works. Rather, we are talking about the cycle of adoption of technology where it really changes the world. The failure, to clarify and characterize it, is *failure of adoption* of the technology. The key point is that if you focus only on your own technology marvel, you may overlook the other factors that are required to make your technology successful in the marketplace. The adoption chain is just as important as the technology— perhaps even more so.

For example, if people hadn't adopted 3G and smartphones, then Uber would not be possible. Segway was focused on delivering its remarkable technology and not on thinking about the ecosystem that would be required to drive successful adoption. That was the mistake and root cause of failure.

The Segway was supposed to change urban transportation forever, but it failed to fulfill its promise despite amazing technology. For all practical purposes, Segway has disappeared from anybody's thought process about the future of transportation.

Uber did *not* have amazing technology, but it did change urban transportation. Ride-sharing has become successful to the point of becoming ubiquitous. Time will tell how successful ride-sharing will be in the long term as a business, but there's no question that we're not going back to the old days of hailing cabs.

Uber rode on the shoulders of core technology innovations that already existed and were widely adopted. People didn't have to be convinced to go out and buy smartphones, and they were comfortable using apps. Other technology companies such as Apple, AWS, and Google invented things that Uber utilized. The company didn't need to make dramatic inventions; instead, it exploited pieces of technology in the ecosystem to deliver compelling customer value. The adoption chain was a force multiplier for Uber but a fatal inhibitor for Segway.

COACHING THROUGH TECHNOLOGY FAILURE

When we create amazing technology, we tend to get invested and excited with it, and we want to make the technology real. However, without the *ecosystem to support the adoption of technology and the support of innovations*, that technology on its own is not as successful. To succeed, you have to look beyond your current technology and execute on it to what else is required to drive adoption and customer value.

Consider the example of autonomous cars, which currently are pushing the limits of technology. At Next47, we have seen a *lot* of autonomous car startups. We were thrilled to see the potential in the technology that makes autonomous driving possible, but it became clear as we dug into it that much more than amazing technology is required for autonomous cars to succeed in the long run. A variety of questions must be addressed to make autonomous cars mainstream.

What are the safety standards? What issues do regulators need to get comfortable with? How safe is safe? Who is responsible for moral hazard decisions, such as when technology has to decide whether to protect the occupant of the vehicle or a pedestrian in the vehicle's path? Will the infrastructure have to be enabled with sensors so that autonomous cars can navigate reliably, and if so, who will pay for it and how long will it take? There are many modes of technology adoption failure currently playing out.

What gets us all excited is breakthrough technology, and I think the world would not be where it is without breakthroughs. The internal combustion engine, the microprocessor, and blockchain all were breakthrough technologies. The important thing to understand is the technology ecosystem. In order for your technology to be adopted successfully, the ecosystem involves who else needs to be on board, how you can empower the ecosystem or position yourself to reduce the risk of adoption failure, and how to enable people to get the full value of the new technology that you're creating.

Breakthrough technology is just the start. There is a long

journey to mass adoption and dependencies that have to be solved for this. "Build it, and they will come" is nothing but wishful thinking. If you allow yourself to be blinded by the brilliance of your technology and narrowly focused on execution in the market, you may fail to consider other innovations required for your technology to succeed.

TECHNOLOGY FAILURE DUE TO ECOSYSTEM: THE WIDE LENS

Some of the best thinking and coaching on technology adoption is in Ron Adner's groundbreaking book *The Wide Lens*. He explains that we live in a world of interdependence where the difference between success or failure hinges on your ability to see, shape, and shift your broader ecosystem. Successful innovators see and solve these dependencies while those enamored with breakthrough technology are doomed to failure.

Before we dig deeper into the coaching in Ron's book, I would like to share my story of how I was introduced to his brilliant work. As I mentioned in this book's introduction, I was fortunate to enroll in his class, "Innovation Strategy and Entrepreneurship," when I attended INSEAD. (He's now a professor at Dartmouth's Tuck School of Business.) Coming from Silicon Valley, I was really excited to learn the best thinking around innovation, and his class came highly recommended by my classmates.

INSEAD used a bidding system to get into classes—it was sort of like a market clearing price. All students were given a certain number of points to bid on the classes they wanted. As I went through the process of deciding which classes to bid on, I kept hearing things like, "If you are at INSEAD, you *have* to take Professor Adner's class—it's the best one you'll take." So I asked him for a quick meeting to explain exactly what material he covered.

When we met, he told me, "My class is a bunch of hype. Don't bid for it—it's not worth the clearing price. I will give you the materials, and you can read them. You don't need to take the class."

Despite his advice, I decided to bid every point I had on his class to make sure that I got in. And I did.

The class was a set of fifteen case studies of companies that innovated and produced, and then every one of them failed. The arc of each case study was, "We've got something really promising here," then "Uh oh—we have all these problems," then "Oh no, we're dead." Ron's great insight across the case studies is not only thinking about the technology and the innovation itself, but also about the ecosystem that enables customers to adopt the technology and realize the promised value. The ideas that he presented in class are further developed in his book, *The Wide Lens.*

In his book, he explains that many leaders have a blind spot when it comes to innovation. Instead of taking a wider view of the entire innovation ecosystem, they are focusing narrowly on *execution*:

> *Yes. Great execution is critical—it is a necessary condition for success. But it is not enough. While this execution focus draws attention to the unquestionably important parts of a company's environment—its management, employees, owners, customers, and competitors—it creates a blind spot that hides key dependencies that are equally important in determining success and failure.*[44]

Numerous companies have fallen victim to this blind spot. For example, Philips Electronics pioneered high-definition television (HDTV) more than thirty years ago and developed many technology innovations along the way. However, the product failed because the other things necessary for Philips's product to succeed—high-definition cameras, transmission standards, and more—were not in place.

As Ron points out in his book, Product Development and Management Association (PDMA) surveys indicate that only about 25 percent of new product development efforts are commercially launched. Of these products that are launched, only about 55 percent meet their product objectives.[45] As he suggests, these failures result not from executive teams executing poorly, but rather not viewing the product ecosystem through a wide enough lens.

According to Ron, to succeed, leaders must widen their focus beyond execution and consider two other specific kinds of risk: *co-innovation risk* and *adoption chain risk*. When you adopt this approach, you are taking a wide-lens perspective on innovation strategy:

- **Co-innovation.** Who else needs to innovate for my innovation to matter?
- **Adoption chain.** Who else needs to adopt my innovation before the end customer can assess the full value proposition?[46]

The way he explained it to us in class was that co-innovation risk is the *probability* of success, while adoption chain risk is the *time* to success.

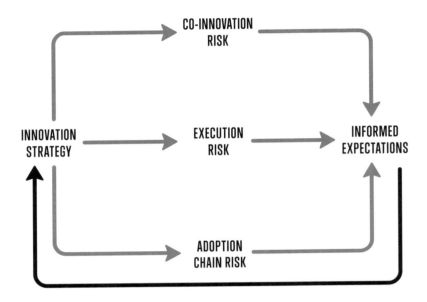

Figure 3-1: The Three Risks of Innovation

In the case of Philips and its HDTV, success required other players in the television industry to develop their own co-innovations—high-definition video cameras, transmission standards, and so on in every step to the consumer. When these co-innovations were not forthcoming, the probability of success for the Philips HDTV set declined precipitously, and the product was doomed to failure. It wasn't until many years later that all the pieces were in place to support HDTV, which eventually became the standard. Either the supporting technology is there, or it's not. In Philips's case, it was not.

In contrast to Philips and HDTV, consider how co-innovation risks played a positive role in the success of Uber. The co-innovations that Uber required for its product to gain acceptance in the marketplace were already in place: smartphones with 3G technology, Google Maps, AWS cloud computing, and so forth. Uber's technology was able to ride on the shoulders of these innovations, thus minimizing the co-innovation risk and increasing the probability of success. If one of these co-innovations had been missing—say 3G technology—Uber would not have been possible.

Adoption chain risk, on the other hand, stood in the way of Segway's success. Many of the cities it was supposed to revolutionize were inhibiting its adoption. There were no regulations in place to support Segway PT riders, and there was no compelling need for cities to accommodate these riders quickly with traffic and pedestrians. Because it was a motorized vehicle, local authorities often did not allow it to operate on sidewalks.

Entrepreneur Peter Shankman, who was among the first five New Yorkers to buy a Segway PT, remembered: "When I first got it, it was so much fun. But the police didn't know what to do with it." According to Shankman, one police officer would tell him to ride it on the street, while another would tell him to ride it on the sidewalk. Yet another officer would tell him he was not allowed to use it on either the sidewalk or the street.

To make Segway scooters work in an urban environment, cities would have to create special riding lanes for them, police would have to be trained to deal with them, citizens would have to be educated, parking would have to be figured out, and much more. The adoption chain had to be dealt with city by city, state by state, and that never would be practical. Even if it was, the time required to bring all these regulatory bodies on board was prohibitive. Segway didn't have enough revenue to sustain its efforts over the long haul necessary to complete this vital task.

When Segway met the real world of government bureau-cracy, bureaucracy won. Steve Jobs was completely off base when he said, "If enough people see this machine, you won't have to convince them to architect cities around it; it'll just happen." As Dean Kamen discovered, no one was prepared to design cities around his invention. In fact, the reaction was largely the opposite.

During a demonstration of the Segway PT that he attended with Steve Jobs and John Doerr, Jeff Bezos wondered aloud, "You have a product so revolutionary, you'll have no problem selling it. The question is, are people going to be allowed to use it?"[47] In some cities, they were not. Prague and Barcelona enacted partial bans on Segways, while San Francisco banned the scooters from sidewalks but allowed riders on streets.

Segway was not only stymied by adoption chain risk, but also by bearing all the costs of co-innovation. These costs added to the product's unattractive selling price, which in turn reduced the number of customers who were willing to buy it. Segways were much more expensive because the original design was complex, and there was no ready supply of off-the-shelf com-ponents. The company had to design and produce everything from scratch and then create a manufacturing chain to produce the scooters.

In contrast to Segway, another company in last-mile mobility, Ninebot, benefited enormously from the ecosystem bearing the costs of co-innovation. Ninebot scooters were far less expensive than Segways because they were much simpler in design, the off-the-shelf components and control units were proven, and the supply chain was already well established. According to Li Pu, former president of Segway Robotics:

Between 2000 and 2012, there was a big change in China. A lot of people in China need to go from their home to work, and they'll stay in a five- to ten-kilometer range. So they have to find a good method of transportation. Before 2000, they were using bicycles. At some point, some of these people started installing electric motors and batteries on their bicycles to create their own electric bicycles. Manufacturers took note of this and started to build electric bicycles for people to buy, and that changed the supply chain for electric motors, batteries, and other components.

By 2005, there were ten million electric bicycles in China.[48] That made the motors, batteries, and control units a mature supply chain. When Ninebot started building electric scooters, it could draw many of these items from the electric bicycle supply chain, cutting development time and costs while increasing reliability and ease of maintenance. Like Uber, the co-innovation risk was negligible.

Ironically, Ninebot acquired Segway in 2015. By then, sales of the original model languished. Meanwhile, Bird, Lime, and other scooter-sharing companies emerged, filling city streets and sidewalks with their two-wheelers and fulfilling inventor Kamen's original dream of transforming urban transportation. Ninebot produced the vast majority of the scooters fielded by these companies. We will see in Chapter 7, "Business Model Failure," that these scooter-sharing companies had their own failures.

TECHNOLOGY FAILURE DUE TO DISRUPTION: THE INNOVATOR'S DILEMMA

Any coaching of technology failure would be incomplete without mentioning the seminal work on technology disruption by Clayton Christensen. His book, *The Innovator's Dilemma*, is one of my favorites because it makes a crucial point: It's not a question of which technology is better now; it's whether the technology meets the market requirements, and the rate at which it's changing and meeting more and more market requirements.

For example, if you consider the successful introduction of the personal computer in the 1980s, it wasn't a question of whether people would buy PCs that were inferior to mainframe or minicomputers at the time. The question was, Are there people who will have uses for the PC, and will an increasing number of people use it? Even though a mainframe was the better technology (faster, more powerful, more storage, etc.), customers had uses for PCs, and they bought them by the millions. Mainframes haven't gone away—it's reported that more than 70 percent of businesses on the Fortune 500 use mainframes—but PCs long ago passed them by in sales.[49]

Christensen's point was eye-opening because the common perception is that the better technology is always going to win. Author Ralph Waldo Emerson is credited for saying, "Build a better mousetrap, and the world will beat a path to your door." Christensen's perspective was that the *inferior technology* can win if it meets market requirements, and it continuously makes improvements. Before he elucidated it, no one thought about innovation that way.

I consider Ron Adner's point just as insightful: Innovations don't succeed based only on execution, but also must address the dependencies on the ecosystem that enable adoption, following the full value chain from the technology to the customer. With his insight, it's easy to see why Segway failed and Uber succeeded.

Christensen and Ron have had a profound influence on my work as a venture investor and a thought partner to founders. I consider them the guardian angels who watch over me and prevent me from falling into the technology failure modes. If you want to avoid technology failure, understand their powerful concepts and apply them to your own endeavors. Then it will be easy for you to see if your own innovation will experience technology failure or succeed.

CHAPTER FOUR

PRODUCT FAILURE

Electric and Musical Industries Ltd. (EMI) was a pioneering British company founded in 1931 to produce both sound recordings and the equipment necessary to record and play them back. The company branched out from those early roots, playing a key role in the invention, development, and production of television broadcasting equipment and cameras, radar, guided missiles, stereo sound recording, and computers.

At the same time as the company created some remarkable technology products, EMI and its subsidiary record labels developed an enviable roster of musical artists, including at one time or another Frank Sinatra, Enrico Caruso, Judy Garland, Nat King Cole, Itzhak Perlman, and many others. However, the phenomenal success of a rock-and-roll group out of Liverpool, England—The Beatles—generated millions of dollars for the company, helping fund initiatives on the technology side of the business. One such initiative was the CT (computed tomography) scanner, first conceived in 1967.

A CT scanner uses X-rays to create images. While a standard X-ray machine is static—creating a two-dimensional image of a structure, say the femur in a tennis player's leg—a CT scanner is dynamic. It uses a rotating, narrow beam of X-rays combined with computer processing to create two-dimensional "slices" of structures. A computer then assembles a series of these slices to create three-dimensional images. One of the first uses of CT scanners was to image the human brain, and today the machine commonly is used to diagnose tumors and bone fractures, guide surgical procedures, pinpoint internal bleeding and other injuries, detect heart and lung disease, and more.

The product was revolutionary when it was announced in 1972, and demand seemed insatiable. EMI had the inventor of the technology on its payroll, it had the patents and intellectual property, the company was flush with resources, and its CT machines were the first purchased and used by hospitals. EMI had the proverbial first-mover advantage. Yet eight years later, EMI exited the CT business altogether.

What went wrong?

EMI—THE FIRST MOVER

For millennia, if physicians wanted to determine what was going on inside a patient's body, they could ask the patient questions about symptoms or feel for abnormalities by hand. If those methods didn't provide the desired results, then the physician would have to cut open the patient's body and have a look—often leading to less-than-optimal results.

This all changed in 1895 when, while conducting experiments with a cathode ray generator, Wilhelm Röntgen discovered X-rays, a high-energy form of electromagnetic radiation. His work earned him the first Nobel Prize in Physics in 1901. Further experimentation led Röntgen to the discovery that X-rays could be used to "see" bones and other structures under the skin. Within a year, X-rays were being used for a variety of medical imaging tasks, from examining kidney stones and swallowed objects to finding bone fractures and bullets in soldiers. The uses seemed endless.

Although the use of X-rays was perhaps the most significant step forward in medical imaging technology, researchers continued to look for better ways to provide the information that physicians needed to diagnose and treat their patients—to look beneath the surface of the skin in noninvasive ways. This is where EMI comes into the story.

Using research and development (R&D) funds provided by the United Kingdom government, along with cash generated from record sales of The Beatles and other EMI artists, Sir Godfrey Hounsfield and his team at EMI Central Research Laboratories invented the CT scanner in 1967. Despite reports to the contrary, EMI gave Hounsfield only about a quarter of the funds he asked for, requiring him to be very creative in his development efforts.

Within four years after EMI began selling its CT scanners, sales were growing at a rate of more than 100 percent a year, and the company achieved a profit margin of 30 percent.[50] As orders poured in, the sky seemed to be the limit.

In the meantime, at least sixteen other companies started to develop and exhibit their own CT scanners, threatening EMI's lock on the market. While many of these new entrants faded away, two global companies with well-established medical divisions, Siemens and General Electric (GE), emerged as leaders in CT technology, introducing their own machines. Demand for EMI scanners peaked in 1977, and sales plunged in the next few years as competitors gained market share, threatening the financial stability of EMI as a whole. In 1980, EMI exited the CT business, selling its EMI Medical unit to GE.[51]

The saga of EMI and the CT scanner is an outstanding case to explode the myth that the first mover, the creator of a product category, is preordained to win. In real life, the *better* product, with a trajectory of relentless and rapid improvement to serve customer needs, ultimately wins. With CT scanners, the winner was Siemens.

SIEMENS—NOT THE FIRST MOVER, BUT NUMBER ONE

Siemens started its own CT R&D unit in 1972, the same year EMI sold its first three production units to the UK Department of Health. Siemens possessed considerable expertise in both electrical engineering, which has to do with safely creating and controlling the high-energy electromagnetic fields that need to be produced, and in mechanical engineering, which has to do with controlling precisely a lot of moving parts. In addition, Siemens had developed some core software capabilities that allowed the company to process the images quickly and make them available and useful for a technician or a doctor to see.

The first Siemens head scanner was named SIRETOM, and it began hospital trials in 1974. The product was a success—it not only advanced the technology, but also demonstrated the potential of CT to physicians around the world. However, Siemens engineers weren't satisfied. What customers really needed was a whole-body CT scanner, which was a much more challenging proposition. According to Andre Hartung, president of diagnostic imaging at Siemens Healthineers, succeeding in the long run requires constantly looking to the future, anticipating customer needs even before they do. Andre said:

> It's very important that you understand what you want to improve in terms of the outcomes. I believe that puts you in an innovation leadership position despite the fact that you may not be the first mover. It's also very important that to some degree you exceed the expectations of your customer. It's great to meet your customer's expectations, but it's even better to exceed them by constantly thinking a step ahead. You identify a problem, you understand the pain, and you try to extrapolate this into the future and understand how it is going to develop.

Siemens's engineers foresaw that when physicians saw the diagnostic power of the SIRETOM CT head scanner, with its capability to look inside the body and see all the soft tissue, there would be immediate demand to have this capability for the entire body. And they were right. In 1977, Siemens introduced its first whole-body scanner, the SOMATOM. At the same time, the company continued to improve its SIRETOM head scanners— improving resolution and image quality while reducing the time it took to do a scan, process the data, and get results. Siemens continued to expand the medical imaging market, while CT sales of first mover EMI declined.

Today Siemens is the number one player in the medical imaging market. Although it was not the first company with a CT head scanner product, Siemens was the first with a whole-body scanner, the first with a heart scanner, the first with a dual-source CT scanner, the first with spectral CT, and so on. The company not only successfully built and marketed CT scanners, but also developed, marketed, and continuously improved many other medical imaging products, including ultrasound, molecular imaging, mammography, angiography, magnetic resonance imaging, and more.

Building a product and nailing product-market fit is a good thing, but even better is securing product-market fit in a market that has many product adjacencies to grow into for second and third acts. While this is not the case for every product strategy, it's important not to rest on your laurels, but to be on the lookout for adjacencies after you achieve product-market fit. The breadth of successful imaging products developed by the company created a variety of advantages for Siemens. Andre Hartung explained:

> As we grew, we built a large installed customer base—I like to call it a fan base. When we have a new product to offer, we know immediately that we have 50,000 customers to go to. They are loyal, and they like us. We were constantly striving to be the innovation leader. And at the same time, we want to have a broad enough portfolio to be a relevant player in an entire space of radiology. If we offered only CT, it would be tough. But having the portfolio we have provides us with an amplification effect.

As EMI demonstrated, it's not the first mover that always wins. It's the company that sees the larger vision and works consistently to create a compelling product experience and to build a record of steady progress that reaches the market potential. It takes more than just a compelling product. You also must have a big vision for the future and a trajectory of improvement that will get you there.

THE FIRST-MOVER HANDICAP

Of course, EMI is not the only company that has proven that first-mover advantage is a myth. The eventual winner in any category anticipates customer needs, starts with a compelling initial product, sees the future opportunity, and executes better than its competition on consistent progress. Let's consider some other notable examples.

SOCIAL MEDIA

Before Facebook became a worldwide social media phenomenon, with more than *2.7 billion* monthly active users,[52] there were MySpace—which was once the largest social networking site in the world—and Friendster. MySpace quickly became an eyesore, an inconsistent hot mess with little structure. Friendster technology did not scale, degrading user experience with long page-load times and frequent service outages. I saw the fundraising pitches of many social networks, such as Friendster, hi5, Snapvine, and so on, but unfortunately not the one that mattered: Facebook.

Facebook leaders took a different approach: curating their social network, building technology properly, improving rapidly to keep up with fickle consumer trends, and measuring impact all along the way. They readily admitted that they did not know what worked, but they continued, consistent with founder Mark Zuckerberg's motto: "Move fast and break things." Then they relentlessly tracked the data on what people actually used, keeping what worked and discarding what did not.

MP3 PLAYERS

South Korean company SaeHan launched the first portable MP3 player in 1997, creating an entirely new way to listen to music. Other companies, including Diamond Multimedia, Compaq, Sony, Samsung, and Creative, soon offered their versions. While these players differed in physical size, memory capacity, and other characteristics, the basic idea was the same: Provide storage and playback capability for digital music files, most commonly encoded in the MP3 digital audio format.

At the time, digital audio files were a new thing for consumers, and record companies didn't sell them. This meant either "ripping" them yourself from music sources (records, tapes, CDs) that you already owned or trading them freely with other people online by way of peer-to-peer services such as Napster, LimeWire, and Kazaa. The quality of the MP3s found on these peer-to-peer music trading sites was not only inconsistent, but also—as the recording industry insisted in and out of courtrooms across the country—the sites were a violation of the music owners' copyrights.

In addition, the MP3 players were notoriously difficult to use. Organizing, navigating, and playing the files—which could number in the hundreds or thousands—was a constant challenge for users who had collected songs in a variety of different naming conventions, levels of quality, and legality. In the opinion of Apple CEO Steve Jobs, they were "too complex. They are really difficult to learn and use."[53]

This all changed when Apple saw the opportunity for everyone to carry their personal music library in their hands and to do it in an elegant, high-quality, and legal way. In 2001, Apple introduced its iPod portable media player to the world. In an Apple press release, Jobs was quoted as saying,

> *With iPod, Apple has invented a whole new category of digital music player that lets you put your entire music collection in your pocket and listen to it wherever you go. With iPod, listening to music will never be the same again.*[54]

I actually saw and briefly used the iPod before the rest of the world did. I was on a cross-country plane ride to Boston, and I happened to sit next to the wife of a senior Apple executive. She had a little white box in her hands, and her headphones were plugged into it. I was curious about the box, and I asked her exactly what it was. She told me the device was top secret but let me try it. I was instantly wowed. A couple of months later, Apple unveiled the iPod to the world.

The iPod was a tremendous success, making other portable digital music players suddenly obsolete or at least decidedly clunky and *uncool*. By April 2007, five and a half years after it went on sale, Apple sold its hundred millionth iPod, making it the company's most successful product to date.[55]

Apple's product vision was not focused on the perspective of an MP3 product, but instead on the user experience of what a music lover would want to have—their hypothesis on the optimal customer outcome. For every product decision—from the initial compelling product to the improvements made along the way—they asked, "How can we make it easy for people to buy legal music?" And they answered this question in a variety of ways.

First, in early 2001, shortly before launching the iPod, Apple released iTunes, a media library where users could organize, collect, and store their music files. In 2003, Apple opened the iTunes Store, which enabled customers to purchase high-quality digital music files legally from all five of the major record labels at the time. Initially, the iTunes Store offered two hundred thousand songs. By 2020, this number mushroomed to more than sixty million songs, along with films, TV shows, apps, and more.[56] iTunes became an ecosystem across its different platforms that tied its hardware together with content its customers wanted and tied customers to Apple.

Second, the iPod design was elegant in what became Apple's trademark white color, its LCD screen was large, and its controls were intuitive and powerful. The iPod's unique scroll-wheel enabled users to navigate quickly through their music collection by playlists, artists, or song titles—with just a thumb or finger. Simply connect your iPod to your computer, and your iPod would be updated automatically with your latest song files.

Third, Apple kept improving the iPod, regularly adding new models to the lineup or moving to new-generation hardware. Capacity and battery life increased, size decreased, and color and other options proliferated.

Today, more than twenty years after the iPod's introduction, the product lives on. Much of the iPod's functionality is built into iPhones or, if you prefer, an iPod Touch, which is essentially an iPhone without the phone capability.

ROBO INVESTING

For as long as there have been investment management firms, there have been human investment advisors who help clients decide where to invest their money. These human advisors usually earn commissions when they make investment transactions— which may skew the advice they give toward investments that will generate more commissions—and they have long been the province of elite, high-wealth clients. Ordinary investors, for the most part, do not have access to the services of these advisors.

What if providing investment advice could be automated, partly or even completely taking the human investment advisor out of the equation?

It can, and it has. In 1996, Bill Sharpe, a Nobel Prize–winning economist, co-founded Financial Engines in Sunnyvale, California. Sharpe won the award for pioneering work in the theory of financial economics and for developing a general theory for the pricing of financial assets.[57] Financial Engines differed from traditional financial advisory firms—it was the first company to focus on robo investing. *Robo investing* is an automated investment advisory service that relies on computer algorithms and advanced software to provide clients with advice and even to invest assets automatically on their behalf.

Financial Engines used the efficient market theory to help build portfolios for retirement plans. According to a brochure describing its services to employees at client Marsh & McLennan:

Financial Engines works with America's leading employers and retirement plan providers to make retirement help available to millions of American workers. Financial Engines is a leading provider of independent investment advisory services for participants in company-sponsored defined contribution retirement plans. Through an agreement with the plans' recordkeeper, Financial Engines helps plan participants with their overall retirement picture by offering personalized retirement plans for saving, investing, and retirement income.[58]

Of course, these "personalized" retirement plans mostly were generated by computers, not humans.

Financial Engines's success with robo investing inevitably attracted the attention of other investment firms, which emerged about ten years after Financial Engines was founded. This new wave of robo investing firms, including Wealthfront and Betterment, saw an opportunity to offer their services to a larger segment of the investing population, improve service delivery, and lower costs. They became popular with the tech crowd, and they continued to refine the robo investing model, making the product easy for clients to use and understand while keeping costs as low as possible.

It's no surprise that the largest financial advising firms soon wanted a piece of the action. Vanguard (Vanguard Personal Advisor Services) and Schwab (Schwab Intelligent Portfolios) became fast followers, putting tremendous amounts of robo investing assets under management. As of 2021, Vanguard had $231 billion, and Schwab had $64 billion robo investing assets under management. The second wave of firms, including Betterment and Wealthfront, lagged behind these market leaders in 2021, with $27 billion robo investing assets under management by Betterment and $25 billion robo investing for Wealthfront.[59] As these companies (particularly Vanguard and Schwab) proved, the best fast followers can win if they deliver better outcomes to customers than the first mover.

And what about the first mover, Financial Engines?

The company was acquired by Hellman & Friedman in 2018 and combined with Edelman Financial Services to create a new company—Edelman Financial Engines—which has been successful in managing retirement assets for employees of their corporate customers. However, when it comes to robo investing for individual investors, the category has new entrants and fast followers leading the league tables.

CLOUD COMPUTING

Utility computing, the idea of paying for computing power based on usage, was the predecessor to cloud computing. It has a long history beginning with IBM in the mainframe era. Starting in the 1990s, companies such as Hewlett-Packard, IBM, Sun, and others began offering various utility computing services. Amazon was a late entrant to the market, launching the Elastic Compute Cloud (EC2) service in 2006. However, none of the first movers have a major share of the cloud computing market today. According to estimates provided by Canalys, as of the fourth quarter of 2020, Amazon's AWS had the largest piece of the cloud with 32 percent, Microsoft Azure with 20 percent, Google Cloud with 7 percent, Alibaba Cloud with 6 percent, and an assortment of other companies with a collective total of 35 percent market share.[60]

Why did the first movers lose their advantage?

Amazon founder Jeff Bezos has a good explanation for why AWS was able to take the lead and maintain it. According to Bezos, the AWS cloud was originally to be used only within Amazon. However, once they realized that other companies would want this service—offloading the capital and ongoing expenditures required to build and maintain their own data centers—Amazon decided to sell it. Bezos explained why AWS gained such a large portion of the market:

> *Then a business miracle happened—this never happens—this is like the greatest piece of business luck in the history of business so far as I know. We faced no like-minded competition for seven years. It's unbelievable....I think that the big, established enterprise software companies did not see Amazon as a credible enterprise software company, and so we had this long runway.... It's just so far ahead of all the other products and services available to do this work today. And the team doesn't let up.[61]*

The failure to recognize Amazon's AWS as a threat was certainly part of the reason why the first movers lost their advantage. Many of the senior leaders I spoke with at HP at that time believed that enterprise customers would never buy from a bookseller. However, not everyone leading large, well-established information technology businesses at the time believed that cloud computing was ever going to amount to anything worth pursuing. At the 2008 Oracle OpenWorld conference—two years after AWS introduced EC2—Oracle founder Larry Ellison had this to say about cloud computing:

> *The computer industry is the only industry that is more fashion driven than women's fashion. Maybe I'm an idiot, but I have no idea what anyone is talking about. What is it? It's complete gibberish. It's insane. When is this idiocy going to stop?*[62]

By 2010, Ellison saw the writing on the wall, and he reversed course, directing his company to build out a broad cloud strategy.[63]

COACHING THROUGH PRODUCT FAILURE

How do you anticipate and avoid product failure? Let's start with first principles, and there is no better example than Steve Jobs and his response to a question at Apple's 1997 Worldwide Developer Conference.[64] The question was about OpenDoc, a product that Apple once championed, but Jobs killed after he returned to the company, first as a consultant and then as interim CEO. The questioner was clearly peeved that Jobs had made the decision to kill OpenDoc, and he wanted to know the rationale. Jobs's response was timeless:

> *You know, you can please some of the people some of the time. But one of the hardest things when you're trying to effect change is that people like this gentleman are right in some areas. I'm sure that there are some things OpenDoc does—probably even more that I'm not familiar with—that nothing else out there does. And I'm sure that you can make some demos, maybe a*

small commercial app, that demonstrates those things. The hardest thing is, how does that fit into a cohesive larger vision that's gonna allow you to sell 8 billion dollars, 10 billion dollars of product a year? And one of the things I've always found is that you've got to start with the customer experience and work backward to the technology. You can't start with the technology and try to figure out where you're gonna try to sell it, and I've made this mistake probably more than anybody else in this room, and I've got the scar tissue to prove it, and I know that it's the case.

You start with the customer, and not just *one* customer. You start with a need that a lot of customers might have. You think about what product and what ease of adoption and what field product features together can serve a large customer population. His starting point for product is *customers*, and it's not just one early adopter who's getting excited about technology. Instead, it's about first identifying the needs of a broad market.

Then he thinks about the product that can serve those broad market needs. This allows him to come back to the initial compelling product that serves the need for a set of customers, then gives them the chance to extend that vision to a very broad audience, keep serving more and more needs, and have a compelling product development trajectory that gets them to this ultimate vision.

Avoiding product failure takes a lot of discipline to stay focused on what matters in serving the needs of a broad set of customers. If you look at the central tenet of how Jobs operated and what he learned as an entrepreneur, the art of innovation with products and doing something big is saying "no" to ninety-nine things so that you can say "yes" to the one thing that will change everything.

Jobs went on to say:

> As we have tried to come up with a strategy and a vision for Apple, it started with: What incredible benefits can we give to the customer? Where can we take the customer? Not starting with let's sit down with the engineers and figure out what awesome technology we have, and then how are we going to market that? And I think that's the right path to take.

The point is that the best way to ensure that your product is going to be a success is to start with what value we can provide to customers now and in the future. Starting with the product, creating it, piling on boatloads of features that engineering dreamed up, and then trying to convince people that they need it is a mistake.

Jobs makes another thoughtful point about "incredible benefits"—the *wow effect*. Notice that he does not talk about a neat technology trick. He talks about benefits or outcomes that are so compelling to customers that they instantly drive adoption—the ROI or value is not in question. For instance, your entire music library in your hands is an instantly compelling outcome or benefit for a music lover.

Jobs also asks, "Where can we take the customer?" He is not necessarily talking about one specific customer, but rather going beyond an early adopter who will try anything to a pragmatic customer who will buy because of the compelling value.

Elon Musk's long-term product vision for Tesla illustrates this point well. Matthew Cowan, general partner at Next47, recalled

hearing Musk's pitch years ago and seeing the company's product vision on a slide. Musk eventually made the contents of the
slide public in a 2006 post on the Tesla blog:

> *Build sports car.*
>
> *Use that money to build an affordable car.*
>
> *Use that money to build an even more affordable car.*
>
> *While doing above, also provide zero-emission electric power gener-
> ation options.*[65]

This is the script that Musk and Tesla have followed all along.
Though Tesla started with the Roadster sports car, which was a
niche early adopter product, their product vision did not end there.
They thought about their product road map to reach the pragmatic customers who make up the majority of the market. And
reach them they did. In 2019, Tesla sold more than 150,000 Model
3s, making it the ninth best-selling car in the United States,[66] and
outselling the perennial favorite, the BMW 3 Series, by more than
3 to 1 in the small and midsize luxury car segment.[67] Tesla also
accounted for 80 percent unit sales volume of battery-powered
electric vehicles (BEVs) in the United States in 2020.[68]

All of this started with the product vision, articulated in Musk's
pitch, almost twenty years ago.

Notice that both Jobs and Musk didn't stop with the early
product and early customers, but kept looking for a path to
broad, mainstream adoption. You may start with a first product
that captivates the early adopter—as Tesla did with the Roadster—because you need to show evidence of customer adoption
and revenue to sustain the company. The initial iTunes store for

the iPod was available only for the Mac. Many startups get into failure mode with products by not thinking beyond the early adopters.

In his book, *Crossing the Chasm*, management consultant Geoffrey Moore describes the gap between visionary early adopters of a product and the pragmatic majority. Visionary early adopters are hungry for big changes and innovations, and they are willing to pay for them. The pragmatic majority, on the other hand, prefers incremental improvements to established products and solutions. The trick to avoiding product failure is to overcome the chasm between these two groups by first focusing on the early adopters and building sales, and once you have a proven product, expanding sales to the pragmatic majority.

It's important to understand that the needs of the early adopters are different than those of the later pragmatists. The pragmatists are the people who one day will compose the vast majority of your market. Like Steve Jobs, you need to have a product vision that—as you're building your product trajectory—includes not only providing what the early adopters want but also anticipating what the pragmatists want. In this way, you can fulfill that broader vision and the broader opportunity for your product.

A lot of product success in the long term is also about execution and fast feedback cycles. Early on in the product life cycle, you might discover that you made some compromises and limitations, and that's natural. You start with the minimum viable product, which allows you to convince customers to buy *and* kicks off the learning cycle. The companies that can refactor their product continually and correct mistakes are going to succeed. If you don't do it, then a fast follower is going to get it done.

Let's look at the evolution of social networks to understand the important of feedback cycles and correcting mistakes by learning from what customers value. If you think about social networks, there were two early social networks: MySpace and Friendster. MySpace ran into a product dead-end of each page becoming completely unattractive for users to spend any time on. It went from people getting excited to being repelled by a lot of garbage pages on MySpace. The company didn't really focus on evolving the product as usage skyrocketed.

Facebook came in behind MySpace. One of the things that Mark Zuckerberg did really well early on was to worry a lot about how easy the site was on the eyes and how easy it was to consume updates from your friends. This was a breath of fresh air compared with MySpace. From the beginning, Facebook attracted the best developers and built the fastest, snappiest social network they could because they knew that fast consumption of the feed was a critically important part of the user experience.

On the other end, you had Friendster, which did not antic-ipate at the beginning the level of adoption that they had. As a result, their technology infrastructure did not scale exponen-tially the way their network scaled. The whole idea of a social network is that you're quickly consuming updates from your net-work. Friendster's technology slowed down the entire site, and it became unusable. Since they couldn't address this technology deck, they didn't retire their technical debt. They didn't refactor. They didn't move from a focus on the early adopter to the prag-matist customer.

Facebook avoided product failure by building learning and feedback cycles into their core DNA. MySpace and Friendster, on the other hand, were trapped by product failure because they didn't evolve their product rapidly enough and didn't continue to deliver a compelling product experience and value the way Facebook did.

Being a first mover could mean counterintuitively that you have a higher risk of product failure. You are going to get all the arrows in your back by being out front in an undefined space while those behind you can learn from your mistakes. If you have the capability to be a fast follower, you're able to avoid the early pitfalls. Google search was not the first search engine by a long shot. But Google had a compelling product and a big vision for the future: To organize the world's information and make it universally accessible and useful. Their search results were simply better (the wow effect), and they were able to maintain that trajectory.

I remember when I tried a Google search for the first time because an excited friend referred me to it. I was weary of search engines at that point—the results were OK, but not that great. One search using Google was enough to have a wow effect on me because the results presented on the first page were noticeably better than other search engines at the time.

Google leaders continue to build on their advantage, and they keep making their product more and more compelling. If you compare the size of the Internet from when Google started to today, it is a testament to their focus on improving their product so that search is still compelling.

Now let me share coaching on avoiding product failure from Gokul Rajaram, currently a member of the executive team at DoorDash and previously a superstar product executive at Square, Facebook, and Google. Gokul brings together in a practical way the ideas we have covered so far: starting from customer value, broad product vision, the wow effect, product building for both early and pragmatic adopters, and the need for rapid learning and iterating. According to Gokul, a product is a beacon that delivers value to customers while driving value to the business. He sees every launch or new feature of a product as a test of hypotheses on quantifiable outcomes for the customer.

The best teams do a good job of articulating the assumptions, hypotheses, and outcomes clearly. They don't think, "Oh, here's a feature. We should launch it." They actually think of a feature as a hypothesis about customer behavior. "Customers will use this product 10 percent more because they'll view it as more useful on this dimension." When there's a divergence, whether it's positive or negative, you should look at the delta and examine your assumptions. Gokul tells how they approached a real-world divergence at Facebook:

> *When I think of failure, I always go back to Facebook. And at Facebook, we had a very successful ad business. [Facebook reported more than $4.2 billion in total ad revenue for 2012.][69] But in 2012, we had this thing called Facebook pages. Facebook pages are these entities that you can create, for example, if you're a writer or a celebrity or the local business—many different categories. Many Facebook page owners didn't want to become advertisers because the process of creating an ad was too complex.*
>
> *So we had an idea: Why don't we make it very easy for the Facebook page owner to create an ad and reach more people? We surveyed them, and we knew a lot of*

them wanted to create ads, but they just didn't have the time. They had the budget, not huge budgets, but there were so many of them, and we felt it was a massive opportunity.

Our hypothesis was that building a lightweight product for page owners to create and run campaigns on Facebook would get some percentage of page owners to use the product and continue to use it. But how do we make it simple? Simplicity was the thing that they all cared about. We somehow conflated simplicity with a subscription product—simplicity means that they shouldn't have to worry about anything; they should just give us money, anywhere from $5 to $10 or $50. We would recommend a budget, and they would just subscribe to it, and then we would take care of the campaigns for them.

We launched that product, and I think maybe a few thousand page owners signed up for it. And then almost everyone who signed up for it canceled their subscription within a month. The churn was incredibly high. Within two weeks, it became clear that this was not going to be a successful product.

Instead of killing the product, we stepped back and asked, "What is it about our assumptions that are wrong? Where did we make a mistake about customer behavior?"

We realized that we had made a mistake because we hadn't gone deep enough to understand what simplicity means to these customers. Simplicity didn't mean subscription. It simply meant they still wanted a lot of control, except they wanted everything to be auto suggestion, auto populate. They wanted to press a button—a one-click option and not a subscription. Money wasn't the issue—they felt they were losing control completely by it being a subscription.

So we changed the product. Instead of making a subscription, we said, "Every time we created a page post, which is a piece of content for a page, we just show everything was populated. We showed here's a budget, and here's how many people you would reach. Just press Submit—that's it." It became an incredibly successful product and an important part of Facebook's ad platform.

The team had a hypothesis, and they built the product, but they admittedly misunderstood the outcomes customers wanted. By going back to the hypothesis with the data at hand, they were able to correct course. If they did not have a hypothesis and did not take time to examine the data against it, they might have prematurely killed what turned out to be a wildly successful product.

These types of deliberate product cycles and feedback loops are the cornerstone of building hugely successful products. We idolize invention, the moment of first creation. However, long-term product success and category victory depend on rapid product evolution that drives improved customer outcomes.

Ultimately, Gokul says, it doesn't matter whether you're the first mover. What matters is whether you're the *last* mover.

CHAPTER FIVE

TEAM FAILURE

Some years ago, a company I worked closely with decided to hire a vice president of marketing as they were reinvesting heavily in their go-to-market after closing a venture round. The founders pinged their network but couldn't find a suitable candidate, so the company's investors suggested that they do a retained search.

The founders specified the kind of person they wanted: someone who could generate leads that would result in measurable sales—not the kind of person who would just create a nice-looking website, place some social media ads, and call it a day. The ideal candidate would be *quantitative* about the approach to marketing, for example, "We'll spend $100,000 on Google ads, which will drive some number of people to our website, and a certain percentage of those people will fill out lead forms, which will result in this many dollars in sales."

The executive search firm went to work—reviewing the qualifications of the most highly qualified candidates and presenting several for the company to consider. After numerous rounds of interviews, the company decided on the best candidate: someone highly experienced in marketing who seemed to check all of the boxes—specifically, having a quantitative orientation to marketing.

With a professional retained search, multiple rounds of interviews with the founders, board members, executives, and others in the company, and rigorous due diligence, how could this key addition to the team possibly fail?

HIRING FAILURE IS A COMMON FORM OF TEAM FAILURE

Unfortunately, this new VP of marketing *did* fail for a variety of reasons. The company's founders wanted someone who would generate leads resulting in measurable sales, and that's what they recruited for. The VP had no problem spending the money but could not consistently deliver measurable returns on the spend. And when the returns *were* measurable, they were not positive. For example, an expenditure of $50,000 on Google ads for the company's products resulted in, say, only $20,000 in sales.

Ultimately, the company's founders realized that their VP had only a couple of plays in the playbook, those plays weren't working, and the VP was not capable of creating new plays from scratch. They realized that the VP wasn't going to change, so within six months after making the hire, they terminated the VP and sought a new candidate who had the numbers-driven focus they were looking for.

They tried the hiring cycle again and failed with another new hire. The person who seemed to be the perfect fit for the job came up short. They never really solved their marketing problem, but they were among the fortunate companies to be clear on what they were seeking and acting early when their new hire did not deliver.

Anytime you hire someone new, you really don't know whether that person will fit into your team and perform at the high standard that you expect. It might be days, weeks, months, or even years before you find out that the person you selected wasn't the right one for your organization after all.

It would be fair to say that scaling the team to match hyper-growth while keeping the quality of talent and performance high is part of the daily grind in any business-building endeavor. Hiring failures happen and are probably the most common type of failure a founder has to encounter. In order for a business to be resilient from team failures, we must start from the very beginning, that is, the founding team.

THE POWER OF A FOUNDING TEAM

Great companies aren't built by lone geniuses. Instead, they are built by incredible collections of talent. The history of business is littered with failures because an inventor could not assemble the critical mass of talent to get the flywheel started or could not scale talent, leadership, and culture to keep up with growth and competition.

I have been privileged to witness a precious few cases where exceptional founders got their teams right. Such was the case at a company called Meraki.

I first met Sanjit Biswas, one of the three founders of Meraki, in June 2009 while I was at Cisco. Also attending the meeting was Bob Friday, who was then the CTO of Cisco's wireless business. Bob previously founded a company of his own, which Cisco acquired, and he eventually left Cisco to start another company, Mist Systems, which was acquired by Juniper in 2019.

During the meeting, Sanjit told Bob and me what he and his co-founders, Hans Robertson and John Bicket, were building at Meraki. Our interest was piqued. The three had met and become friends while they were graduate students in the Massachusetts Institute of Technology's computer science program. Sanjit and John were in the PhD program, and Hans was in the master's program.

Around 2005, they had the idea that they could commercialize some of the research they and others were doing at MIT. They decided to go to a few banks in the Boston area and ask for a $60,000 loan to get started. The bankers kept enquiring whether they were going to start a pizza business. This was puzzling to them until they realized that their loan amount was approximately what a commercial pizza oven typically cost back then!

The original idea was to build out a Wi-Fi mesh network, first in Cambridge, Massachusetts, and then take the system to other places in the world. The system would be based on inexpensive radios linked together to provide Wi-Fi coverage in a community. With this product idea in hand, Sanjit, John, and Hans founded Meraki in 2006.

When we first met with the Meraki founding team, they were still focused on building rooftop municipal mesh Wi-Fi systems, and that market was going nowhere. They realized this, but they also knew that their products had tremendous potential. They were taking wireless and merging it with cloud computing, which was emerging at that time. They built a wireless system that was incredibly easy to use and manage. They made the decision to pivot to mid-market customers, just below the core enterprise market where Cisco played.

Sure, the product was interesting, but Bob Friday and I could sense that Meraki's team was really special. We knew they eventually would find the right go-to-market motion for the company and be successful with it, no question. I remember what Bob said to me as we left the meeting: "I can smell something big here." This was a company that we would have to find a way to work with, invest in, or acquire. Indeed, Cisco did acquire Meraki in 2012. I believe that today Cisco would consider Meraki to be its most successful acquisition of all time, based on the multi-billion-dollar business that Meraki has become.

What exactly did Meraki do right with teams?

The first thing was the starting condition of the founders' complementary strengths important to business building. John and Sanjit had earned some of the highest research honors while doing their PhDs at MIT. John in particular was a technology genius—he had the chops to build something amazing on his own or with a small team. In this case, they built the foundations of mesh network technology. It was almost as if they had rewritten all of the Cisco networking stack on their own in a few months.

Hans brought an incredible capacity to understand and scale product and go-to-market. You could see that he had started to figure out what the go-to-market motion was that actually would work against Cisco if they made the shift from municipal to enterprise. He thought about how Meraki's product would differ from Cisco's product and how they could combine this product and go-to-market in a way that would notch customer wins.

Sanjit had an ability to frame the broader vision, to get investors bought in and excited about the story, and to recruit great people into the organization. As it turned out, he also enjoyed doing hardware design—deciding what components and chips they would use for their different products.

These three brought together the complementary strengths that each one of them could not bring on their own. They crossed the biggest hurdle in team failure by starting with an incredibly strong founding team.

The founders were modest, but they had an intensity that was off the charts. Each one of them in turn built out their teams in a way that attracted talented people to join them. They decided they would focus on hiring A+ players, and they hired for attitude, not necessarily experience, which enabled them to build a truly outstanding team.

The founders recruited their first team members from MIT, attracting a handful of exceptional computer science PhDs to the company. The quality and reputation of this core group set the pace for Meraki to keep bringing high-quality engineering talent in the door. I have seen this pattern again and again with successful startups: The best talent you can assemble initially comes from your own network. If you can't convince the best people in your network to join early, you have a problem. The Meraki team crossed the second hurdle in team failure by attracting the core early team that was a force multiplier for the founding team.

Hans previously worked at EMC as a product manager, and he studied other companies at that time and how they built their sales teams. You could see that he had built a sales engine of people who were extremely motivated. They didn't recruit people who worked at Cisco, and they didn't recruit people from channel partners that sold Cisco's products. Instead, they deliberately went after high-performing salespeople in other areas—for example, selling copiers—and they taught them how to sell networking. They were looking for what you would call athletes, and Hans was able to bring these athletes together, teach them how to sell a strong network product, and then scale the team. They were fearless and focused: The team competed hard and won against a dominant 70 or 80 percent market share incumbent.

To be successful with Meraki, you had to give more than 100 percent, and you had to be totally committed. You could not hide. The way that John ran the engineering team as it scaled was to keep splitting the team and the tasks into smaller chunks. He never would manage a team of fifty people—he always managed teams of seven, eight, or ten people with discrete tasks. As teams grew and then split, he promoted people to manage them.

The same went for sales. Meraki never had a blob of a team with performance that they couldn't understand. This was no small feat because it's often challenging to understand performance as you're scaling. However, Meraki was able to keep the granularity and visibility of individual employee performance. When someone didn't perform, they could weed out the employee and prevent a so-called bozo explosion. This is when you hire a low performer, let the person fester, then they hire more low performers—bozos prefer to hire bozos—and it becomes a drag on overall performance. The Meraki founders crossed the third hurdle in team failure by not allowing complacency and underperformance as the team scaled rapidly.

Another thing Meraki did while growing was being disciplined about not overtitling or overcompensating their new hires. They not only looked for very talented people, but also looked for people with a lot of runway or room for growth in the organization. While the Meraki team crossed the fourth hurdle, having a high talent-to-title ratio, I have seen the opposite with many other start-ups. Such overtitling usually leads to team failures when people become unworthy of their early ranking as the business scales.

In summary, Meraki avoided many common team failure modes while building an incredible team and scaling their business rapidly behind the power of this team. Yes, they started with incredibly talented founders, and they built amazing new technology that allowed networks to be managed from the cloud. But they succeeded because of the high-quality team they put together to build their business.

TEAMS WIN IN THE LONG RUN, NOT THE LONE GENIUS

When people think about the creation or invention of some new technology or product—especially a technology or product that becomes the basis of a transformative company—they often put their focus on one person. They might, for example, associate the emergence of the automobile industry with Henry Ford, or the invention of light bulbs with Thomas Edison, or the tremendous success of Apple Computer with Steve Jobs, or the global growth of Facebook with Mark Zuckerberg.

This is a mistake. While these individuals were instrumental in creating the inventions or companies they are associated with in the minds of the public, they didn't work alone. Each created a remarkable collection of talent, working together to achieve lofty goals.

Although Steve Jobs *was* Apple for many outside observers, he would admit that this was not the case at all. Sure, Jobs's vision of the future set Apple's direction. But he depended on teams of talented people to turn his remarkable vision into reality. Said Jobs in an interview with *Time* magazine more than two decades ago:

> *So what I learned early on was that if you could assemble a team of these very high-performance people, extremely talented people, a few things happen: Number one, unlike what you'd think, they actually all got along with each other. This whole prima donna thing turned out to be a myth with the very best people. Secondly, small and medium-sized teams of these people could accomplish extraordinary things and run circles around large teams of normal people. And so I have spent my work life trying to find and recruit and retain and work with these kinds of people. My #1 job here at Apple is to make sure that the top 100 people are A+ players. And everything else will take care of itself.*[70]

When I think about remarkable collections of talent, one of the best examples in Silicon Valley is the group known as the "traitorous eight." This was the group of eight people—Julius Blank, Victor Grinich, Jean Hoerni, Eugene Kleiner, Jay Last, Gordon Moore, Robert Noyce, and Sheldon Roberts—who left Shockley

Semiconductor in 1957 to form their own company in Mountain View, California: Fairchild Semiconductor. It was here that members of this team invented the first true monolithic integrated circuit—the foundation of modern-day computers.

The true greatness of the traitorous eight was not recognized until much later when team members spun off and did great things elsewhere. They became the de facto startup incubator for Silicon Valley, directly or indirectly creating many other companies and sparking many other technologies and even venture capital. In 1961, Jean Hoerni, Eugene Kleiner, Jay Last, and Sheldon Roberts left Fairchild to join Amelco, which was then owned by Teledyne. In 1968, Gordon Moore and Robert Noyce left Fairchild to form NM Electronics, quickly renamed Intel. Eugene Kleiner eventually went on to found venture capital firm Kleiner Perkins Caufield & Byers, which funded numerous Silicon Valley startups, including Google, Sun Microsystems, Netscape, Genentech, and others.

In some cases, a lone genius assembles a talented team, for example, the animation team put together by Jeffrey Katzenberg at Disney that produced some of the company's most enduring films, including *The Little Mermaid*, *Beauty and the Beast*, and *The Lion King*. Sometimes teams serendipitously come together and do great things, like the traitorous eight. But regardless of how they come about, achieving the right balance within the team—and maintaining it over time—is key to the long-term success of any organization.

How do you build such a remarkable collection of talent? What does this team look like? How do you harness its members for long-term success? And how do you keep up with the hypergrowth that results?

Let's start with the basics. When you're in business-building or startup mode, you're going to double or triple the size of your organization every year. The job description of a team member you hire today probably will be different six months from now. Someone may be brought in to manage one product, and six months later they may manage ten people and three products, and then it's going to grow from there. When you're hiring, you need to have plenty of runway or headroom.

Ideally, people grow with the company. But if they don't grow, you need the headroom to bring in others who will take you farther. The person who took you from $1 million to $10 million in revenue in a sales role may not be the person who takes you from $10 million to $100 million in revenue. If you don't overpromise and overcommit, that allows you to bring in talent who will be right for the next phase of growth. It takes finesse to do this in a way that is seamless and doesn't bruise a lot of egos along the way. Managing those expectations during the scaling process is a big part of getting it right. Not managing the situation when someone in the team hits the ceiling is a common form of team failure.

It's important for leaders and teams to keep in mind the next person they're going to recruit that is better than they are in some dimension. If you're running cloud engineering, how are you going to hire the next cloud engineer on your team who is better and knows more than you? That's how you strengthen your company, your bench, and your capabilities. If you are recruiting people who are *not* better than you in some ways, then your organization is not going to be able to scale, and you hit another form of team failure.

As venture investors, we encounter situations where one of the founders serves as CEO, another runs go-to-market, and the third runs engineering. If all three don't scale equally and at about the same rate of speed—say if the engineering lead turns out to be more of an individual contributor than a team builder—then the founding team needs to have the courage to bring in someone else who can keep up, or even better, drive growth. Successful business building is not about making everyone feel good but letting it fail in the larger purpose.

Finally, no new business, startup or otherwise, can afford to recruit people into key positions who are learning the basics on the job. Having top talent with both skills and runway in every key leadership role in a company is critical. Although it's tempting when you are an early-stage company to imagine your first team learning on the job and leading to greater heights, that's usually the wrong idea.

Mike Speiser and Sutter Hill Ventures have a unique model, which is to work with talented technical founders to imagine the next great product that needs to be built. Mike or one of his partners then incubate that first team in their offices, and a partner serves as the first CEO. Mike, for instance, will serve as the founding CEO of three or four companies at a time. When the company is ready to fly, he'll go out and recruit the real CEO, then step back.

Next47 partner T. J. Rylander said, "What that ensures is the quality of the CEO who takes the helm of these companies, and in turn the quality of the initial team that CEO is able to attract. We see it repeatedly, and what Mike and Sutter Hill do is nothing short of a superpower. He thinks of these products, and then he helps the companies get going, leading to outstanding outcomes." The most recent great outcome was Snowflake, which he served as the first CEO and in September 2020 guided the company through the biggest initial public offering of a U.S. software business ever.[71]

TALENT WITH PURPOSE

To build a team that is going to succeed in the long run, you have to build it with a purpose in mind. If there are people on that team who cannot help you get to that purpose, you must have the courage to step back, reassign, or remove the people who aren't aligned with it, and bring in the team that's going to achieve it. If your goal is to win the championship, you have to recruit and retain people who share the dedication to winning the championship.

That doesn't mean that you hire a team of prima donnas—that's not the point at all. The point is that there's a commonality of purpose, and there's a commitment to do the hard work to get there. That's what we've done here at Next47. Siemens gave us a purpose, and we said, "OK, what can we do with the team to achieve that purpose? Let's bring in people who are aligned with that purpose and committed to it and who will pursue it with zero supervision."

The last thing a founder can afford to do is spend time trying to convince people who are not aligned with the purpose to pursue it. Chances are they won't.

When you're building teams with purpose, there are many paths to success. There isn't a single formula that always will succeed, and the way the sales team is managed and nurtured might be quite different from the way the engineering team is managed and nurtured. The people you hire may have different philosophies when it comes to how they approach their jobs, and that's OK.

It's a little bit like a football team. You have offense and defense, and you might work them differently. That's fine. In terms of culture, the subcultures that might exist in an organization, and the motivations of team members, I think there are a lot of variances in business building.

Assembling talent with purpose, special skills, domain expertise, and drive is more critical than ever as business cycles today continue to accelerate. The generalist manager model that is left over from conglomerates is dead. One day, a generalist is supposed to manage airplane engines, and the next day, manage financial services firms. That model of success may work in a purely steady state or a financially oriented conglomerate, where it's just the question of managing scale. But it falls down when you're building a team with purpose—when you're inventing a new category, and you're trying to move much faster and be much better than the incumbent. The only way you can do that is to bring strengths in your area and constantly add to them while connecting with the overall whole and the purpose for building the team.

COACHING THROUGH TEAM FAILURE

As you work to avoid team failure, it's important to remember that founding teams with complementary strengths are most likely to change the world. The ideal founding team's ingredients are product vision, technical chops, and missionary selling. It's the founding team and early team members who set the culture and destiny of the endeavor. Great people want to work with other great people whether it is product, engineering, sales, marketing, or operations. One unaddressed bozo can cause a bozo explosion.

Because the most successful new business ideas grow at two or three times a year, the business may quickly outgrow the capabilities of the early team. Do not overtitle, overcompensate, or overpromise early on, making it difficult to bring in the right person for a different scale of the company. The hardest conversations are with one of the founders who is not scaling. Acquiring talent and establishing culture are good problems in a rapidly scaling business. Getting them right is as important as getting the product and selling motion right.

Let's look at some particularly instructive approaches to coaching through team failure.

THE SCORE TAKES CARE OF ITSELF

One of the people I really admire for the quality of the teams they've built is Bill Walsh, the fabled head coach of the San Francisco 49ers football team. When Walsh arrived in 1979, the team was widely considered to be the worst in the National Football League, with a record of two wins and fourteen losses in 1978. Walsh soon turned around the team, and the 49ers went on to win the Super Bowl three times during his ten years as head coach. In addition, Walsh was named NFL Coach of the Year twice during his tenure, and he racked up an enviable winning percentage of .609 (92-59-1).[72]

Of course, Walsh didn't accomplish these feats all by himself. He found great people—players, coaches, and staff—and put them in the positions that brought out their full potential. As Walsh explained in his book, *The Score Takes Care of Itself,* "Running a football franchise is not unlike running any other business: You start first with a structural format and basic philosophy and then find the people who can implement it."

However, every team, business or sports, has superstars as well as people who aren't as accomplished. It's up to leaders to focus their coaching on the people on their team who most need it and to remove those who don't have the capacity or capability to perform at the required level. Said Walsh in an interview in *Harvard Business Review*:

> Take a group of ten players. The top two will be supermotivated. Superstars will usually take care of themselves. Anybody can coach them. The next four, with the right motivation and direction, will learn to perform up to their potential. The next two will be marginal. With constant attention, they will be able to accomplish something of value to the team. The last two will waste your time. They won't be with you for long. Our goal is to focus our organizational detail and coaching on the middle six. They are the ones who most need and benefit from your direction, monitoring, and counsel.[73]

While Walsh's record as head coach of the 49ers is what earned him a place in the Pro Football Hall of Fame, I believe his greatest legacy is the remarkable team of players and coaches that he assembled. Like the members of the traitorous eight who left Shockley Semiconductor and went on to spark numerous Silicon Valley startups, many of those recruited by Walsh went on to accomplish great things—both while they were part of the 49ers and in their careers afterward.

On the player side, Walsh drafted and developed compelling players in almost every position on the team, including Joe Montana at quarterback; Jerry Rice and Dwight Clark at wide receiver; Ronnie Lott, Eric Wright, and Carlton Williamson at defensive back; Jesse Sapolu at center; Roger Craig at running back; and many others. Walsh looked for special people and put them in positions where they could maximize their talent. You can't attract special people if you don't give them the space to express their talents. Everybody's working toward the same common goal, but you need to provide these special people with an environment where they can be themselves and bring out their full potential.

However, it was Walsh's coaching tree—the assistant coaches he developed and influenced—that puts him in the top ranks of the NFL's greatest coaches of all time. This tree contains at least thirty-one NFL head coaches, including Mike Holmgren, Sam Wyche, George Seifert, Jim Fassel, Dennis Green, Mike Shanahan, Jeff Fisher, Brian Billick, Jon Gruden, Steve Mariucci, Gary Kubiak, John Harbaugh, and others.

Walsh's approach ties back to building teams with a purpose. I believe that you can't be successful in a startup if you don't build this set of complementary talents—who are deep in their areas, but also working together for a whole. You can't bring in a bunch of generalists who don't have depth because they will not be able to attract people who are even smarter than themselves, specializing in the right areas. The virtuous cycle of deepening talent in the bench will be neither sparked nor sustained.

BETTER TOGETHER

In his book, *Collaboration*, business professor Morten Hansen makes the point that the best leaders aren't solitary geniuses who ride in and save the day all by themselves. Instead, the best leaders are those who are collaborative and who harness the collective intelligence of their teams. In an interview, Hansen explains why Apple beat Sony in the MP3 player market:

> *In 2001, Steve Jobs introduced the iPod for the world to see. The slogan was "1,000 songs in your pocket." In reality, it was a combination of many existing pieces into a very cool product, enabled by collaboration inside and outside Apple. Now think about it; who should have launched that product and owned the market for portable music players? Sony, with its history of the iconoclastic Walkman! And they tried. In 2003, Howard Stringer, the U.S. head of Sony, decided to launch a counterattack by drawing upon the vast resources they already had—a music division, the VAIO computer line, the Sony Walkman, hard-disk players, and online music stores. The problem was Sony did not have a culture of collaboration among the divisions that needed to work together to make this happen. They simply couldn't collaborate effectively. The result, a product called Sony Connect, was so bad that it didn't get any traction and was eventually killed in 2007. Although other factors than collaboration played a part, Sony gave up the market they had invented to Apple because they failed to collaborate.[74]*

In an article they wrote for *Harvard Business Review*, Joel Podolny and Morten Hansen assert that the change in organizational structure instituted by Steve Jobs after he returned to Apple as CEO in 1997 was key to the company's ability to foster collaboration and ultimately innovation. According to the authors, in a single day, Jobs laid off the general managers for all of Apple's business units and put the entire company under a single P&L. Then the functional departments of the company's business units were combined into a single functional organization that aligned expertise with decision rights. As they explain, "Relying on technical experts rather than general managers increases the odds that those [product] bets will pay off."[75]

When you build a team that is collaborative, you'll get the best out of everyone on it. It's a situation where 1+1 really does equal 3.

ANTICIPATING TEAM FAILURE AS YOU SCALE

When your company is growing rapidly, that is not the time to try to learn on the job. It's a better time to encourage your young talent to grow, but to bring in the right balance of experienced professionals who can show how it's done. The time will come for your younger talent to pick up the reins, but first they must gain the experience they need to grow and succeed. If you don't take that approach, and you're not looking at how quickly the key people in your organization can grow, then you're falling into a team failure mode. However, you can anticipate and avoid that as you scale.

A common failure mode begins when one of the co-founders does not scale along with others on the founding team. These are hard conversations to have in startups—no one wants to tell their college buddy that they're not delivering in the key role. The rest of the management team can see it, but no one does anything about it. Just because you were successful up to some point in the company's growth doesn't mean that you will continue to be successful through hypergrowth. You can't afford to risk the failure of the entire team and the company by letting key people learn on the job.

As Next47's T. J. Rylander pointed out, there are certain elements of leadership that scale naturally. "This includes product vision, the ability to motivate your team and to bring everybody along, and the ability to engage with outside stakeholders to tell the story. Because if you can tell a story to one person, you can tell that same story to a thousand people and can always set the hook." However, other elements of leadership don't scale naturally, mostly functional roles such creating a go-to-market strategy, building compensation plans for your sales team, or working through the mechanics of at-scale product delivery. These are roles where experience really matters.

If you are a founder—employee number one—you are going to be the source of the vision and the product brilliance, and that can be the case forever. However, you probably are not going to be the source for how to scale a sales team to reach $1 billion in revenue. That's where you need to bring an experienced executive to lead the charge—whether it's building the sales team or a multi-product engineering team that can deliver on time with high quality. If you've never done that before, now is not the time to try to learn on the job.

Finally, it's important to recognize that there are many more potential sources of team failure than the ones we focus on in this chapter. Building a new business is extremely intense, and it's not advisable for someone who has significant life events or emotional issues that would be exacerbated by this high-pressure environment. In addition, issues such as work-life balance and burnout, conflict between team members, lack of diversity of views, geographical and time zone differences in a distributed team, and more can take their toll on individuals, teams, and ultimately the organization. Be on the lookout for these kinds of negative issues within your team—and yourself— and be ready to act when you find them.

CHAPTER SIX

TIMING FAILURE

In March 2015, I met with Andy Rubin at Voyageur du Temps (French for Time Traveler), a Japanese bakery that he and his then-wife created in a hundred-year-old former train station in Los Altos, California. They imported chefs from Japan to make the bakery's European-inspired pastries, and the architecture was distinctly Zen minimalist. However, what was distinctly *not* Zen minimalist were the fingerprints of Android everywhere you looked. The waiters were all taking orders on Android devices, and the cash register was an Android tablet.

That should be no surprise since Andy is the founding father of Android, placing him in the pantheon of Silicon Valley luminaries. Despite all his accomplishments, in later years Andy was revealed as not a good actor—on and off the job.

When I arrived, he led me to a private meeting room at the back of the bakery, with a view overlooking the Foothill Expressway, which is where the train tracks used to run until they were decommissioned and replaced with asphalt in the early 1960s.

Andy had just left Google, where he served as senior vice president of mobile and digital content, and he was creating a venture fund and startup studio called Playground. He was in the process of raising $300 million to create a unique place where amazing hardware, software, artificial intelligence (AI), and compelling design would all come together. He also was assembling a coalition of companies around the idea of creating the future of smart devices.

By the time we talked, he already had Foxconn, which manufactured much of the world's smart devices, committed to Playground. He had Google behind him, with all the software and the cloud chops in the world, along with their extensive mobile experience. He was talking to Hewlett-Packard because they were a very important player in the PC and devices markets, and they brought a well-established distribution network to get the devices into customers' hands. He also was speaking with large semiconductor makers and mobile operators, completing the ecosystem on which to launch smart devices.

During our meeting, Andy shared that he had an ace up his sleeve. The ace was a new smartphone, eventually called the Essential Phone, designed to challenge Apple and Samsung, at the time the dominant players in the smartphone market. In fact, he was not content just to challenge Apple and Samsung; his plan was to reinvent the smartphone and make a product so compelling that people would switch to his new one.

Here was a groundbreaking product, developed by the person who invented the super-successful Android OS (used by 85 percent of smartphones worldwide),[76] backed by ample capital, world-class talent, and some of the biggest names in technology. The timing seemed opportune since Apple and Samsung had plateaued on must-upgrade features from generation to generation. What could go wrong?

THE ESSENTIAL PHONE— NOT SO ESSENTIAL

Andy Rubin is a technology pioneer. A computer science graduate, he eventually found his way to Apple, where he worked as a software engineer. When Apple spun off General Magic, which was pioneering an early version of the smartphone, he went along to help create the company's Magic Cap operating system, which eventually powered the Motorola Envoy and Sony Magic Link devices. After General Magic folded, Andy co-founded Danger, Inc., which developed the Danger Hiptop smartphone, sold by T-Mobile as the Sidekick.

He went on to co-found Android, where he developed the open-source Android OS. Google acquired the company in 2005 for an estimated $50 million,[77] and the operating system proliferated into all sorts of digital devices, including watches, televisions, game consoles, digital cameras, and more. As of 2019, there were two and a half billion active Android devices worldwide, and there are likely many more than that today.[78] Andy remained at Google for more than nine years before he left to found and become managing partner of Playground, which is where he was when I met him.

If anyone was going to reinvent the smartphone, it was going to be Andy, which made people want to be a part of whatever it was he had up his sleeve.

When the Essential Phone was introduced in 2017, it was similar to other smartphones but different in some interesting ways. Andy's idea was to make the smartphone modular so that accessories such as a three hundred sixty-degree camera or a headphone jack adaptor could be magnetically clipped on and quickly paired with the smartphone, removing hardware limitations. The phone was going to ship with a pure version of Android in partnership with Google, with the aim of overtaking Apple, Samsung, and other smartphone producers.

The Essential Phone was all about increasing the hardware and software choices for the consumer and having a compelling design, with a durable titanium body sandwiched between a large, edge-to-edge Gorilla Glass screen and mirrorlike ceramic back. As one reviewer commented, "That mirror finish. It immediately reminded me of the monolith from *2001: A Space Odyssey*. I just had to touch it."[79] The potential upside was huge, and the company earned a valuation of more than $1 billion even before it shipped its first unit.[80]

However, Essential did not ship very many units after the first one.

The phone originally was scheduled to ship in June 2017, but this was delayed twice before units actually began shipping at the end of August 2017. Once units began to ship, customers were decidedly underwhelmed. The Essential Phone lacked the kind of standout features that would separate it from the well-entrenched competition. In fact, despite its beautiful exterior, things weren't so great inside the device. As a review of the phone on CNET explained, "Essential's camera still isn't competitive. T-Mobile reception can be problematic. Battery life is merely OK. No photo or video stabilization. No headphone jack. Essential's modular camera is a battery hog."[81]

In addition, Rubin signed a deal with Sprint to be Essential's exclusive partner on release of the phone, a move that was hoped to increase the product's visibility. And while it was OK for Apple to sign an exclusive agreement with AT&T when they introduced the iPhone, that playbook was not appropriate in a more mature smartphone market. That late in the game, the Essential Phone would have had a better chance of selling if it had been available through every carrier and every retailer to put it in the consideration set for mainstream customers.

As it turned out, the Essential Phone wasn't so essential after all. Press reports put sales at five thousand units through Sprint in the first month after release,[82] and research firm IDC reported that the company shipped a grand total of eighty-eight thousand units in 2017, even after prices were slashed in an unsuccessful bid to attract customers.[83] To compare, Apple sold its millionth iPhone only seventy-four days after it was introduced in June 2007.

After unsuccessfully looking for a buyer for the company, Andy Rubin announced in February 2020 that Essential would be shut down.[84]

We all know the old saying, "Timing is everything." And while timing might not be *everything*, it is certainly an important part of the success of any business venture. Introduce your new product or service too early, and customers won't be ready for it. Too late, and the battle for market share in a new category may already be over, and the barriers to entry too high.

In the case of the Essential Phone, it was clearly a case of delivering too little, too late. Despite the stellar team and partner ecosystem assembled by Rubin, and all the capital raised, the actual product was not the great leap forward as advertised. The value proposition that Andy offered in this mature market was not sufficient to compel Apple and Samsung phone owners to switch, so they didn't, and Essential failed.

THE APPLE NEWTON

Long before the failed Essential Phone, and even before the wildly popular Apple iPhone, there was something called the Apple Newton. In 1985, after ongoing conflicts with Apple CEO John Sculley, Steve Jobs was pushed out of Apple. After Jobs's departure, Sculley focused on growing the Macintosh personal computer business while he tried to figure out what the next computing platform would be after the personal computer. That product turned out to be the Newton—the first personal digital assistant (PDA), a term coined by Sculley—which began development in 1987.

James Joaquin described what it was like work on the Newton development team, which he joined in 1990. James is co-founder and managing director of Obvious Ventures, and he previously served as president and CEO of both Xoom.com and Ofoto. He and I were colleagues at a venture firm for a period after he left Xoom. James said about his introduction to the Newton:

> *I was originally recruited by Apple to run an engineering team because I had a particular programming specialty, and they needed someone who knew that*

*math and programming technique. Not long after that,
Michael Tchao approached me and said, "Hey, I want
you to come interview for my team. We need a product
manager with a technical programming background."*

The interview took place in a top-secret Apple skunk works on Bubb Road in Cupertino, a couple miles away from Apple's headquarters. There were no signs on the building to indicate that it had anything to do with Apple and it had its own security guard. The team working on the Newton was called the Advanced Products Group, and it was made up of some of Apple's best and brightest, including Jerome Coonen, software team lead from the original Macintosh team; Steve Capps, a legendary early Mac team engineer; and Larry Kenyon, who built the networking stack for the original Mac. James was offered the job as product manager of the operating system and developer tools, and he accepted.

Sculley had already come up with some ideas for what kind of device might one day replace the personal computer, specifically, something called the Knowledge Navigator. Presciently, the Knowledge Navigator took the form of a foldable tablet that opened like a book, used a touchscreen for input, and had an intelligent voice assistant to interact with and anticipate the needs of users—not unlike Apple's current Siri. It had a calendar, could make and receive video calls, and could send and receive email messages. In addition, it could access a digital network of university libraries, combine files, print documents, and more. Sculley even commissioned mockups of the device, which he presented in a video during a 1987 keynote.

But Knowledge Navigator was just a concept—a balsa wood model, vaporware. It would take a lot of R&D and engineering horsepower to build a product that resembled anything close to this vision of Apple's future.

The Advanced Products Group accepted the challenge and began development of the Newton PDA. This required reimagining *everything*. For example, if the future of computing was going to be portable and mobile, then the device would need to be battery powered. And since no suitable battery existed at the time, Apple would need to build their own battery lab and invent a new battery. As a result, the central processing unit (CPU) would need to be very low power to avoid depleting the battery too quickly, which meant that the team could not adopt the standard Motorola chips used in the Mac. They would need to invent or partner and find a reduced instruction set computer (RISC) chip from ARM, a brand-new company at the time.

The team decided that instead of a keyboard, the Newton would use a touchscreen and handwriting recognition stack that was very computationally intensive, and they decided to invent a new networking paradigm using diffuse infrared. Whenever anyone came into a room with a Newton device, they all would instantly link together, creating their own wireless mesh network. In addition to all that, the Newton would need its own unique operating system to run everything seamlessly.

In parallel with the development of the Newton, a different team in Apple was working on a similar project, also blessed by Sculley. The project did not receive much attention from Apple management, however, and it was spun off in 1990. The resulting company, General Magic, was co-founded by Bill Atkinson, Andy Hertzfeld, and Marc Porat. The sketch of their idea for the Pocket Crystal "remotaphonputer" looks remarkably similar to the iPhone, introduced to the public in 2007. After spinning off General Magic, Sculley pushed forward with the Newton—putting the two organizations in direct competition. According to James:

> *There was this really interesting rivalry between General Magic and the Newton team. Originally, the Newton team was going to build this tablet—it was like a slate. Think iPad. And the General Magic team was going to do this very small, pocket-sized thing. Think iPhone. I think at the time John Sculley thought, "These are two separate bets. This one we'll spin out, and the other one we'll do internally." And then, what ended up happening was that the two teams converged in a head-on collision—both coming to the conclusion that you couldn't do large-screen device because it looked too much like a laptop, and the market would expect it to run Lotus 123 and WordPerfect.*

While the Newton team was focused on producing an Apple PDA, they also were busy signing hardware OEMs that would embed the Newton OS into a variety of products, creating a huge ecosystem—in much the same way that Android has been embedded in all sorts of products well beyond smartphones. Apple was highly motivated to make the Newton a success because they anticipated that PDAs would grow into a multi-trillion-dollar market—much bigger than the personal computing market.

As development of the Newton progressed, numerous issues had to be addressed. An advanced microprocessor had to be developed (the ARM6 chip was used), the infrared networking function had to be tweaked (it consistently failed in the presence of fluorescent lights, the standard in most businesses at the time), and the software had to be debugged (the seven hundred fifty thousand or so lines of code contained thirty-seven hundred bugs a month before the software was supposed to be delivered to Sharp to be embedded in units as they were manufactured).[85]

After six years of development, the Apple Newton MessagePad finally was offered for sale in August 1993 at a price of $900. James was part of the team that launched the product in Newton, Massachusetts (no coincidence). While the Newton initially attracted much interest with consumers and the tech press (fifty thousand units were sold in three months), there were problems with the hardware and software. The Newton's processor ate AAA batteries like candy, and its handwriting recognition software was famously buggy—so much so that the Newton was made fun of in the popular *Doonesbury* comic and on *The Simpsons*.

Improvements were made, issues addressed, and new versions of the Newton put on sale. Handwriting recognition was greatly improved, RAM was increased, faster processors were developed, and rechargeable battery packs were developed. However, sales were tepid—only between 150,000 and 300,000 units were sold within the four and a half years after the first Newton was offered for sale.[86] In February 1998—a year after he triumphantly returned to Apple—Steve Jobs killed off Newton. Said Jobs at the time, "This decision is consistent with our strategy to focus all our software development resources on extending the Macintosh operating system. To realize our ambitious plans, we must focus all of our efforts in one direction."[87]

What happened? Why didn't Newton become the tremendous hit that John Sculley imagined it would be? In retrospect, it's obvious that Newton was a product that was ahead of its time. Aside from the hardware and software issues that initially plagued the product, customers weren't yet ready to buy a computer that fit in the palm of their hand. Customers loved the idea of a pocket-sized smart device, but they didn't need or want it to do all the things that Newton did—and they didn't want to spend $900 for it.

What customers *were* ready for was something much less capable and much less expensive. They found this in the PalmPilot 1000 PDA, which was introduced in 1996 at an initial price of $299. It focused on doing just four things, and it did them well: calendar, contacts, notes, and calculator.[88] Like Newton, the PalmPilot 1000 relied on handwriting recognition for input, but its Graffiti software worked better than the handwriting recognition software used in Newton.

The PalmPilot was a huge success, selling 1.6 million units in 1998—a 57 percent increase from the previous year.[89] Where Newton was ahead of its time, PalmPilot was exactly the right product at exactly the right time. While we could attribute some measure of Newton's fate to the customer failure concepts discussed in Chapters 2 and 3, the ultimate outcome was mostly a result of timing failure. James Joaquin recalled:

> *Even though Newton and General Magic had way more funding and all these brilliant people, the PalmPilot team said, "Forget all that—forget about travel agency in the sky with a new platform. Let's just build something simple that just takes your PC stuff and puts it in*

your pocket—a companion to your personal computer."
And that's what the market was ready for, that's what
it was asking for. The thinking at Apple was we knew
what was best for the customer. We knew the future,
and we were going to just reverse engineer from that
future and show consumers why it was so great. But
we were so steeped in stacking all this n-squared risk
that we misjudged the distance from the present to the
future. We were directionally correct, but we were 10
years off. That's too large a margin of error for build-
ing a business.

While the Newton was a tremendous failure for Apple, when
the company introduced the iPhone in 2007, it got the timing
exactly right. It wasn't the first smartphone, but it turned out to
be the best—providing customers with the exact suite of features
they were looking for at a price they were willing to pay ($499
for the 4GB model).

TWO CURVES TO GET TIMING RIGHT

What is it that separates the trajectories of the Newton, iPhone,
and Essential Phone over the course of three decades? In a word,
timing. Fundamentally, there is a right time for building massive success in a new business. That means there are many, many
wrong times. Since none of us has a reliable crystal ball that will
tell us when the right time is, we need to look at the data. There
are two curves at work that determine whether the timing of
your new venture is going to be right or wrong.

The first curve is technology capability at cost points attractive to the market. Newton was too early for the market—the

technology capability and unit cost weren't there yet. We discussed technology failure in more depth in Chapter 3, and we can see Ron Adner's co-innovation and adoption risk at play with the Newton, too. When Newton was introduced in 1993, the Web was relatively new, and few people or companies were using it—there were only one hundred thirty websites in existence that year. That number jumped to about three thousand in 1994, the year Yahoo! was founded.[90] Wi-Fi had not yet been invented. 3G phone networks didn't exist.

For a new product to be successful, different technology capabilities have to come together at a price point that meets the wallet of enough customers to make the business model work.

The second curve is market readiness. While you might have the technology capability to do some task—for example, to store your photos on a mobile device—if people aren't used to the idea of taking a digital photo, then they aren't going to buy a phone to take photos. The Newton preceded the commercial launch of the Internet, so e-commerce did not yet exist. People were not using the Internet to do activities such as booking travel, storing their documents, sharing photos, or connecting with their friends. If people aren't used to booking airline or sporting event or concert tickets online using their desktop computer, then they're unlikely to buy those tickets on their mobile device. The market just wasn't ready for the services the Newton was designed for its users to enjoy.

For a product to be successful, these two curves—technology capability at an attractive cost and market readiness—have to intersect. And when these two curves intersect, a window is created where it is the right time for a new product to come to market and for the company that introduced it to build market share.

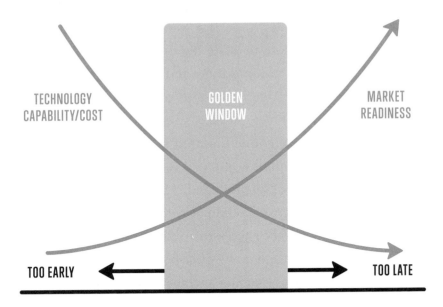

Figure 6-1: The Golden Window

In the case of the Apple Newton, which was released before the window opened, the company could not nail the technology capability, and consumers were just not ready for it. The ultimate product was buggy because it was stretching the edges of technology to the limit, it was expensive, and it did far more than customers wanted it to. And in the case of the Essential Phone, which was released after the window closed, the incumbents were entrenched, and there were no new technologies or customer needs that redefined the curves. New entrants are simply not able to create a new category to offer anything compelling in terms of doing something that wasn't done before or in terms of serving a completely unmet market need that didn't exist before.

The golden window of opportunity for smartphones was from 2000 to 2010. This was when all the technology and connectivity—as well as customer readiness and usage of the

Internet—intersected beautifully, and that's where the category leadership battles were fought. When you are coming in before a window like this opens or after it closes, you're simply not in a position to win a significant market position. Every category of tech product has its own golden window of opportunity—from MP3 players to smartphones to enterprise Software as a Service (SaaS) to social networking to cloud computing.

Let's think for a moment about the golden window for cloud. Today we can see this play out with the adoption of cloud by enterprises. Until recently, most large enterprises maintained their own data centers, which meant they had to buy or lease their own computing hardware, then buy the software to run on it, plus hire the people to do all the required tasks to maintain and secure these systems. Cloud computing eliminates much of this, enabling organizations to pay for only the amount of computing resources they need and to be assured of having the best technology available.

However, the cloud could happen only when interconnectivity and network bandwidths were high, when the underlying hardware technologies could be commoditized, and when the underlying operations for maintaining the hardware and software could be standardized. Google and Amazon built their own internal clouds out of necessity to serve their search and e-commerce customers at competitive unit economics. Only then could cloud happen for enterprise customers, and when it did happen, it eliminated a lot of the complexity for the customer—creating a golden window of adoption. And as we can see with cloud, it's hard for new entrants to stake out space in the industry now that there are entrenched incumbents such as AWS, Azure, Google, and Alibaba.

While timing may not be everything, it's an important consideration when you're introducing a new product or service. Get the timing right, and you'll maximize your chances of success. Get it wrong, and you may have to anticipate failure.

IDENTIFYING GOLDEN WINDOWS

What if you could have a crystal ball that told you in advance, with 100 percent accuracy, the perfect timing for the introduction of your new product or service? Unfortunately, no such thing exists. However, certain founders, executives, and management teams have developed a sense for where markets and technologies are headed, and their companies and shareholders have benefited as a result. John Chambers, former executive chairman and CEO of Cisco, and the talented team he assembled there were devoted practitioners of the art and science of seizing golden windows.

John served as Cisco's CEO for more than twenty years, growing the company from annual revenues of $70 million when he took charge to $47 billion when he stepped down.[91] I worked at Cisco from 2009 through 2011, and I had a chance to see him and the Cisco leadership team in action. I believe that much of Cisco's success was a result of its management team's ability to see and seize windows of opportunity—what Chambers called *market transitions*—and take advantage of them well before competitors. According to John:

> *A market transition occurs when there is a subtle but clear disruptive shift. It could be social, economic, or technological, and it begins many years before the market actually grasps its significance and adapts to it. A market transition gives you a glimpse of a new*

opportunity to take market share or move into new market adjacencies, and it can take many forms. For instance, it could be a process shift, like the shift to open-source software.[92]

It's this window of opportunity—which is at the intersection of technology, customer needs, and economics—that creates a period of rapid adoption of an innovation by the market. In an interview in *Harvard Business Review,* John gave the example of the transition of phone networks from Public Switched Telephone Network (PSTN) to Voice over Internet Protocol (VoIP), which he predicted in the mid-1990s. The Cisco team could see that within about five years, traditional telephone companies—which were built on proprietary telephony technology—would lose between 80 and 90 percent of their revenue as companies and people migrated to VoIP networks. And John didn't hesitate to warn the leaders of two major telephone companies what he saw coming: "Your primary revenue stream could almost completely disappear," he told them. "You need to move to other services and other capabilities to replace the disruption enabled by voice over IP."

Although the technology was not yet in place when John made his prediction, he could see that it was on the way. Why would people continue to pay to access proprietary telephone networks when they could transmit VoIP networks for free? It was just a matter of time before the necessary technology would be in place, and Cisco would be there, ready and waiting. John said:

We saw customers across the board beginning to shift away from proprietary networks, like IBM's Systems Network Architecture (SNA), toward Internet Protocol–based networks. They were voting with their dollars, even though bandwidth was pretty limited then. We applied Moore's law to networking to predict what IP networks could be capable of five years from that point. We saw that if a router could support a kilobyte today, it could support a megabyte tomorrow. And when that happened, we believed, everything—not just data, but things that had never gone over IP networks, like voice and video—would be connected to the Internet.[93]

Those people who didn't understand the intersection of technology, customer needs, and the economic curves didn't anticipate the transition of voice from proprietary networks to VoIP networks. John Chambers and Cisco did, and they cashed in on it, building a multi-billion-dollar business. According to John and consistent with what I observed, if you are able to anticipate this window of opportunity, when the time is right, you can build a billion-dollar business in five to seven years, and sometimes with consumer businesses, you can build it even faster. These windows of opportunity are appearing faster and faster because business cycles are faster, and new entrants are relentless in prospecting for new windows to open so that they can either create a new category or beat an incumbent.

It can be difficult for incumbents to react and to get their response right when market transitions occur—particularly when these transitions are the result of a platform change. John Chambers got the transition to connected mobile consumer devices wrong when he championed the acquisition of Pure Digital, maker of the popular Flip pocket-sized digital video cameras. A story has it that he anticipated the transition intuitively when he saw everyone in his family pull a Flip device out of their pockets during Thanksgiving celebrations. Right after

Cisco acquired Pure Digital, Apple launched the iPhone 3GS, which had video recording built into it. Overnight, the Pure Digital business deteriorated, eventually leading Cisco to exit the consumer business.

While Cisco and John at least saw an opportunity and acted on it, the behavior of many incumbents, such as Larry Ellison and his denial of the cloud in 2008, as discussed in Chapter 4, is to deny or to recognize too late that the platform changes are happening. They are so successful on the existing platform that they don't want to believe that a wholesale move to a new platform could take place, giving new entrants an advantage by starting from scratch. As a result, these successful startups took advantage of timing with respect to platform changes: Salesforce was Siebel in the cloud, Instagram was Facebook on mobile, and iPod was the Walkman for digital music.

The concept to understand from all this is that when the technology capability and market readiness curves intersect, and you are in this golden period, *that's* the time to place your bets. Whether you are an entrepreneur or a large company, you have to understand that this is the time when market share and market dominance will be established.

COACHING THROUGH TIMING FAILURE

What steps do you take to identify market transitions and take advantage of them? And conversely, how do you avoid timing failure by being too early or too late?

Let's say you're a large company like Cisco. First, you must have the radar out there to watch for these golden periods of market transitions. When you see something coming over the horizon, you must recognize that this is the time when market incumbents and losers will be established, and when customers will be willing to switch. Therefore, this is the least expensive time to gain market share. It's this concept, I think, that established companies have a hard time understanding and an even harder time pursuing.

If you are a startup or an entrepreneur, then you're going to be willing to invest a lot in this type of window—even suffer heavy losses. You know that, in spite of all these losses, if the customers you acquire are valuable, and this is the only window where you can acquire them, then you can get a lifetime of profits from them. But if you think it's expensive to acquire customers now, consider that it's going to be orders of magnitude more expensive to get them to switch later. Also keep in mind that many of them will never switch because the switching costs accumulate to gargantuan levels.

If you're a large company, you've got to watch out for market transitions that are happening in your core or adjacent markets. You also must accept that you have to make your bets at that time, in that market, when that adoption is happening. If you miss that window, you risk going extinct or being unable to compete in that opportunity.

If you don't have the capacity to compete early on, then you have to make a commitment either to acquire another company that's already in the market or to invest heavily in customer acquisition and product development. If you feel right about that market transition, then you're going to reap the rewards on the other side when you can build a billion-dollar business in the five-to-seven-year window that John Chambers talks about.

When you do that, you'll be positioned to dominate that market as it grows. It's essential not to be slow in either recognizing or acting on these market transitions.

Facebook provides several good examples of seeing a market transition and acting on it. At some time, there was a tipping point where everyone carried a camera in their pocket—their smartphone. That trend combined with the rollout of 3G networks created a golden window where people increasingly communicated with photos. Kevin Systrom and Mike Krieger saw this golden window, and they co-founded Instagram in response. Within a year, Instagram had ten million registered users.

Facebook was already deep into the photo business—they were the largest repository of photos at that time—so they couldn't afford to lose. Mark Zuckerberg reportedly worried that because many Instagram users exported their photos to Twitter, the teamwork of Instagram and Twitter could threaten Facebook's dominance in social media. Facebook was working on a mobile photo app, but its internal data science team clearly could see that Instagram's adoption was on an exponential trajectory. Zuckerberg was so concerned about the potential threat to his company that he decided to act. In 2012, Facebook acquired Instagram—a company with just thirteen employees at the time—for an astronomical $1 billion in cash and stock.[94] Although this was a high price to pay, by 2018, Instagram was estimated to be worth more than $100 billion.

Facebook faced a similar situation with messaging. For decades, when people wanted to converse, they would pick up the phone and make a call. However, people started bypassing the phone networks altogether in favor of SMS and other messaging apps. Facebook saw this market transition coming and created its own messaging app, Facebook Messenger. However, WhatsApp was gaining more messaging traffic than Messenger, causing Zuckerberg to be concerned that WhatsApp could beat out Facebook in messaging. Again, his internal data science team confirmed his fears. In 2014, Facebook acquired WhatsApp for $19 billion.

We know now that Facebook's actions were prescient in seizing the golden window, but might have fallen within the gray zone of antitrust laws. These are extreme examples of market transitions, but they show what happens when a company is willing to pay whatever it takes to win the competition and not wait to suffer the consequences as the golden window passes them by.

When drone startup Skydio, a company in our portfolio, was started in 2014, the founders were a bit early in the golden window. Their first product, the R1 autonomous drone, was consumer focused and meant to compete with popular products such as those sold by DJI. The drone attracted tremendous attention in the press and with consumers because of this autonomous capability. That feature was best in class—no one else's technology came close. Over time, they kept improving this unique capability, managing their burn, and staying patient until the golden window opened for them. In the meantime, many drone startups disappeared as they burned through capital too quickly. Now Skydio is thriving in the golden window, building drones specifically for the enterprise market, where they are used to do all sorts of tasks, from public safety and emergency response, to remote inspection, defense, and more.

Skydio is a case where the technology capability was ready, but the company had to wait for the market to arrive, creating the golden window that they enjoy today. They had staying power—selling consumer products while they improved their autonomous technology and then developing enterprise products that now form the largest share of the company's sales. When the golden window opened, Skydio was ready.

At Next47, we recognize market transitions by speaking with the people who are deep into how technology capability and market readiness curves intersect. That's the reason we like to back product-focused CEOs and founders. They're always asking: "What's possible now that wasn't possible before?" They're constantly experimenting, tinkering, and creating something. It's like eBay founder Pierre Omidyar saying, "Now that there are a bunch of people on the Internet who have stuff sitting in their garage they want to sell, maybe I can create a platform that enables them to do that." Or it's like former Ofoto CEO James Joaquin saying, "Hey, wait a second. Maybe people want to keep all their digital photos online and print from there instead of going to the corner store to have them printed."

The way to get ahead of this is to keep speaking with these people. If you speak with enough of these people in new areas who are experimenting with new kinds of products, then as an investor you're able to see whether this new product capability is hitting the mark with customers. You can tell this is happening when the customers let go of whatever things they were using before and start to lean in and buy this new thing. It's more than likely you're going to get a market transition wrong, but the way we as venture investors do it is to work with founders who have this product vision—who are seeing how things can be different in the future, creating something that can be put in front of customers, and observing the reaction.

Sometimes you get it right, and sometimes you get it wrong, but hopefully more often than not you'll get it right. When it happens, you'd better be there to establish your footprint and play in that market with customer adoption because if you take three years to figure out what your strategy is, the golden window has closed, and you're dead.

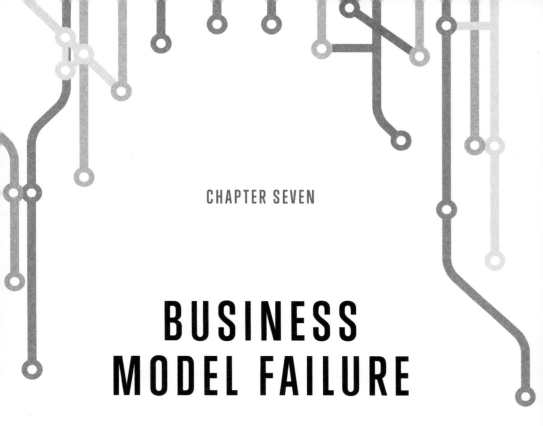

CHAPTER SEVEN

BUSINESS MODEL FAILURE

As you can imagine, my team at Next47 and I are on the receiving end of a lot of startup pitches, and we are scanning the market constantly for interesting new startups and founders with breakthrough ideas. While few of these ideas ultimately pan out, every once in a while, one offers the promise of tremendous upside to change the status quo meaningfully.

In July 2017, I attended the Fortune Brainstorm TECH conference in Aspen, Colorado. During the conference, I had a conversation with Davis Wang, CEO of Mobike, that left me buzzing with excitement. Based on our discussion, I was excited about the idea that urban mobility was on the cusp of radical change. Just minutes after talking with Davis, I sent the following email message to the Next47 team:

You will be interested in this data point. At the Fortune conference today, I met with the CEO of a Chinese bicycle-sharing company called Mobike. They launched in April 2016. Today, they have 100 million users, 20 million active daily users, 6 million bikes, and are active in 160 cities, including a handful outside China. Talk about scaling a business at startup speed! In January 2016 they were worth $20 million; now they are raising money at a $2.6 billion valuation.

Partnering with founders who plan to change the world is a calling for us at Next47. For Mobike to generate such tremendous growth in a little over a year was a rare feat, a true outlier. We needed to learn more about this new industry and whether we should invest. By July 2018, a year after I wrote my email message, China's bike-sharing companies had grown at an astonishing speed, with the two market leaders, Ofo and Mobike, each accounting for more than two hundred million users in nearly one hundred seventy Chinese cities.[95] This begged the question: Would bike-sharing take off in the United States? Was this going to be the next big thing?

As it turned out, bike-sharing did *not* catch on in the United States. What did catch on was something similar: *scooter*-sharing.

The first scooter-sharing company on the scene was Bird, founded in 2017 in Santa Monica, California, by Travis Vander-Zanden, who previously served as COO of Lyft and then as vice president of global driver growth for Uber. VanderZanden decided that the future of *micromobility*—the term for short-distance transport using electric scooters or bicycles—would be in scooters, not bikes, and he made that the focus of his company, Bird Rides (later shortened to Bird). In September 2017, the company placed its first ten scooters on the streets of Santa Monica, officially sparking the scooter-sharing craze.

This craze gained momentum for a couple of reasons. First, the scooters were *fun*, and people were excited to check them out. Second, using the product was easy. Simply download the app onto your phone, set up an account and payment, find a waiting scooter, and off you go. The early momentum drew investors to this promising, new business like a big flock of hungry...*birds*.

As we researched the emerging scooter-sharing landscape, Next47 general partner Matthew Cowan personally met with the founders of several companies. According to Matthew, Vander-Zanden successfully pioneered the market because of some unique insights:

> During his tenure at Lyft and Uber, Travis was able to observe the general distribution of rides. His first point of brilliance was the realization that a very significant percentage of these companies' revenue came from short-haul rides around downtown metropolitan areas. His idea was to create a lower-cost form of transportation that would focus on this sweet spot in the market. His second point of brilliance was identifying a form factor that was easy to use, accessible, novel, and seductive. As a result, scooters really caught fire.

Within a year after Bird sent its first ten scooters into the wild, the company logged more than ten million rides, expanded to more than one hundred cities, and became the fastest startup in history to achieve a valuation of $2 billion.[96] It was a unicorn on steroids. Lime wasn't far behind, making the shift to shared scooters in 2018 and quickly logging millions of rides for its product. According to an exuberant McKinsey, in 2019, its models indicated that the micromobility industry would surge to between $300 billion and $500 billion by 2030.[97]

The micromobility market was on a tear, with no end in sight. Until all of a sudden, it wasn't.

The number of global shared and private micromobility passenger-kilometers traveled in 2020 declined precipitously— between 60 percent and 70 percent. The pain felt by the industry worldwide as a result of this shift in rider behavior was real. As a more sober McKinsey reported:

> *The valuation of one company operating a worldwide network of e-bikes and e-scooters recently dropped by a reported 79 percent. Another provider halted operations in six U.S. cities and all of its European markets, laying off 30 percent of its workforce. A third company cut working hours for 60 percent of its staff while supplying a streamlined fleet of its e-scooters to health care workers in Germany.[98]*

What happened to those many millions of electric scooter riders? What happened to Bird and Lime and all the other companies that stoked the micromobility market? What happened to the potential $500 billion industry?

A HUGE INVESTOR MAGNET

As with many other venture capitalists, the micromobility market was squarely on our radar screens at Next47 in mid-2018. We had seen the massive growth in dockless bike-sharing in China that had taken place in 2016 and 2017—I had visited

China during that time to explore this and other opportunities. By 2018, however, the wheels were coming off the dockless bike market in China.

Chinese streets were littered with piles (in some cases, *mountains*) of unused bikes. Many bikes were vandalized or left unrepaired, and margins were thin. Within a year after launching its bikes in thirty U.S. cities, Ofo was forced to exit most of those cities and lay off staff in the United States. When Bird and Lime emerged in the U.S. with their shared scooters, the opportunity looked quite attractive.

We were concerned that the market might mirror the sudden rise and decline of China's bike-sharing industry. But it couldn't be denied that the adoption rate for scooters in the United States was remarkable. As Figure 7-1 shows, ride-sharing was one of the fastest-adopted consumer technologies ever—significantly outpacing smartphone adoption when it was first launched. However, as shown in Figure 7-2, scooters blew other forms of ride-sharing out of the water, being adopted at 6x the rate of ride-sharing in the early days. This meant that the early signals were exceptional for the potential of scooters to be the next big thing in consumer technologies.

When you take a very top-down, blue-ocean strategy perspective, you are fundamentally saying, "Go into an uncontested market space and create a different value curve with your offering." The data we had seen seemed to indicate that micromobility was a blue-ocean market with tremendous potential for future growth.

A small detour on blue oceans: The idea of a blue-ocean market comes from one of my personal favorite business books, *Blue*

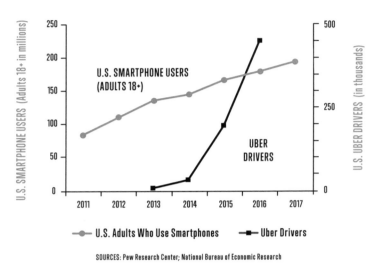

SOURCES: Pew Research Center; National Bureau of Economic Research

Figure 7-1: Rate of Adoption of Ride-Sharing versus Smartphones

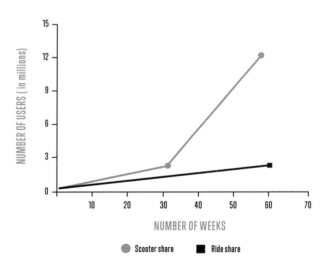

Figure 7-2: Rate of Adoption of Scooters versus Ride-Sharing[99]

Ocean Strategy, written by W. Chan Kim and Renée Mauborgne while they were professors at INSEAD. According to the authors, *red oceans* comprise the industries and markets that currently exist. They are well known, the rules that govern them are clear, and there are few surprises—risk is relatively low. As this existing market space becomes increasingly crowded, competition gets fiercer, and profits are squeezed until the products become commodities. This is the case for many industries today, including retail banking, airlines, computers, and so on.

Blue oceans, on the other hand, are industries and markets that do not currently exist. Few know or understand what these industries and markets might be in the future. The rules are for the most part unknown, and there is great uncertainty as well as relatively high risk. But these blue oceans can have tremendous potential. Consider the example of ride-sharing pioneer Uber, founded in 2009. The industry did not exist in its current form before Uber created it. The company's market cap at the time of this writing is $84 billion.

Now, back to Bird and Lime. If you look at the concept through the blue-ocean framework, it is beautiful. You can draw a curve that shows an existing form of transportation, has a certain entry price, offers certain benefits, and serves certain segments of customers. Since you're going into a fundamentally uncontested space, which previously was served primarily by automobile ride-sharing platforms such as Uber and Lyft, this is a fantastic top-down strategy. It's compelling as a hypothesis, and it checks the box from a blue-ocean strategy perspective.

However, while the market opportunity might look compelling, it still needs to check the three boxes we discussed in Chapter 2. There has to be a viable hypothesis about a customer problem, a viable hypothesis about what product or service you're going to offer to solve that problem, and a viable business model. If you zoom in on the business model, what we're really talking about is *unit economics*—a profitable transaction for the person who actually is solving the problem. As we dug deeper into the dockless e-scooter opportunity, we began to have our doubts.

As the adoption curves in Figure 7-2 show, customers clearly were interested in using dockless e-scooters. The scooters were convenient—faster than walking and in some locations, faster than a car. They reduced the hassle of owning and maintaining your own scooter or bike, they were readily available when and where users needed them, and they did not have the carbon emissions of cars. In addition, they were less expensive than taking an Uber or Lyft ride and comparable to the price of public transportation such as buses. The product and technology were well established and readily available. Bird initially used consumer scooters built by Chinese companies Xiaomi and Ninebot, which we met alongside Segway in Chapter 3.

The problem with scooters was in the business model. More specifically, we had concerns that the unit economics of e-scooters would not provide for a viable long-term business model. In retrospect, our concerns appear to have merit.

When we first looked at the unit economics of scooters in mid-2018, we met with more than twenty different micromobility-related companies to gain insight into the industry. Based on our initial research, the unit economics looked compelling. Another insight that Travis VanderZanden gained while at Lyft and Uber was that one of the greatest challenges for unit economics and profitability in the automobile-based ride-sharing industry was the driver. Despite the fact that they were considered independent contractors and not employees, drivers were a significant expense. By removing the drivers, the scooter-sharing unit economics models looked much better than automobile-based ride-sharing models. Figure 7-3 shows what we and other observers at the time saw.

UNIT ECONOMICS

REVENUE PER RIDE		
Charge per ride	$1.00	Same across all vendors
Charge per minute	$0.15	Same across all vendors
Average ride length	20	Estimated minutes
Revenue per ride	$4.00	

COST PER RIDE		
Maintenance cost	($0.21)	Assuming maintenance every 14 days; costs $20/maintenance
Charging costs (user)	($0.21)	Assuming 30% of scooters are charged by the user; 7 rides per day per scooter, costs $5 to pay the user to charge a scooter
Charge costs (vendor)	($1.50)	Assuming 70% of scooters are charged by the vendor; 7 rides per day per scooter, costs $15 for the vendor to charge
Cost per ride	($1.92)	
Profit per ride	$2.08	

Figure 7-3: Unit Economics for Scooters (July 2018)

We calculated the revenue per ride to be $4.00 and the cost per ride to be $1.92, making for a net profit of $2.08 per ride. As it turned out, we weren't getting the full story of what was really going on. According to Ching-Yu Hu, a partner at Next47:

> *A core part of our diligence was focused on a company's fully loaded unit economics, including the depreciation line—oftentimes, we would see companies not include this in their analysis. Scooters at the time cost about $400, $500 and were essentially identical to the consumer scooters that you could buy online. They weren't designed for 10, 15, 20 rides per day, so the lifetime of these scooters turned out to be a couple weeks to a couple months at best. As a consequence, the short vehicle lifetime directly resulted in a more dramatic impact on the depreciation line, which significantly impacted profitability. Additionally, the market was highly exposed to seasonality. We would sometimes see companies cherry pick and highlight cities where they were profitable without context on the profitability of their operations across geographies. One of them chose Paris, for example—which was doing really well and showed positive unit economics—while 95 percent of their cities were negative.*

When we dug deeper into the unit economics, we discovered that there was a mirage when we were looking at profit on a per-ride basis: both the revenues and the costs were deceptive to some degree. We gained much greater clarity when we started looking at the entire ecosystem for an entire day, not just per ride for an individual vehicle. Figure 7-4 shows the updated unit economics for scooters based on this new approach, which we presented in March 2019.

UNIT ECONOMICS

Key levers are the vehicle cost, useful lifetime, charging operations, and maintenance.
Achieving a positive contribution margin remains elusive to all competitors.

REVENUE PER VEHICLE PER DAY		
Trips per vehicle per day	4.10	
Revenue per trip	$3.80	
Gross revenue per vehicle per day	$15.58	Pricing per ride: $1 to unlock, $0.15/min, 18 min avg ride length
Discounts/promotions/refunds	($3.58)	
Net revenue per vehicle per day	$12.00	After discounts/promotions/refunds

COGS PER VEHICLE PER DAY		
Insurance fees	($0.10)	
Payment fees	($1.40)	Players are moving toward pre-paid wallets to lower these fees.
Network platform	($0.50)	
Depreciation	($5.20)	Assumes scooter costs $570; useful life of 4.5 months.
COGS per vehicle per day	($7.20)	
Gross profit	$4.80	
% of net revenue	40%	

ADDITIONAL COSTS PER VEHICLE PER DAY		
Juicers	($6.60)	Freelance gig workers who change, rebalance scooters nightly; several players exploring fixed charging stations.
Local ops / maintenance	($3.90)	Vandalism, loss, theft, and hoarding are rampant. Players are realizing mechanics need to be FT not contractors.
Customer support	($0.30)	
Additional costs per vehicle per day	($10.80)	
Contribution margin per vehicle per day	($6.00)	
% of net revenue	(50%)	

Figure 7-4: Unit Economics for Scooters (March 2019)

The big thing people were not getting right in the unit economics was cost.

The first thing affecting cost was the reliability or the useful life of the scooter. People made assumptions that these scooters could last for five or six months. What actually happened in the wild is that many scooters stopped working within a month or two after they were deployed. They were consumer-grade scooters, and their useful life was not as long as many people expected.

The second thing affecting cost that people didn't get right was that the scooters had to be located in the right places, and they had to be charged. This meant relying on a network of freelancers who were supposed to pick up the scooters, charge them, and then put them back onto the street. The scooter companies had to pay the freelancers to provide this vital service. As the companies grew, they couldn't find enough reliable freelancers. They had to pay a premium to recruit enough people to charge the scooters and put them in the right place every night.

The third thing affecting cost was theft, abuse, and vandalism. People were holding onto these scooters, keeping them at home, and not making them available for others. Some people found scooters to be annoying, and they dumped them into trash cans or bushes. Yet others were abusing or breaking scooters by overloading them with riders or by crashing them.

Where people originally thought they were making $2 of profit per ride, in reality each scooter was on average bringing in total revenue of $12 a day. However, the total costs were actually $18 a day per scooter, so they were losing $6 per day per scooter, which was massive. This business model was unsustainable without significant changes in either the revenue side or the cost side of the equation—or both.

When venture capital investors see massive adoption, such as what we saw with scooters, we are willing to pay for a period to do experimentation and to fund early growth. The explosive growth of scooters was being driven by the availability of cheap capital—almost a billion dollars of capital for Bird and Lime together—not to mention all the money previously raised in China for dockless bikes.

However, there comes a window of time where people have to figure out whether a particular business model is a money-making proposition or not. What was becoming clear was that on the cost side, the dockless scooter business was not a money-making proposition.

After you look at cost, the next challenge to consider in unit economics is revenue. Can this truly become a mass market of the magnitude people were expecting? Will regulatory barriers be put in place that will hamper growth? Are safety issues going to cause potential riders to decide not to use the product? These were some challenges to be considered on the revenue side.

There were increasing numbers of stories in the media about people seriously injured and even killed riding scooters. Many riders didn't wear helmets or other protective equipment. These safety concerns capped the growth beyond the early adopters who were young and nimble, and who were used to riding non-motorized scooters in their youth. It really was not a mass-market, every-commuter-in-every-city type of proposition, so concerns about safety were a drag on the industry going to scale.

City and local governments were growing increasingly annoyed with the number of scooters in their streets and on their sidewalks. Some cities implemented regulations on the number of scooters that could be deployed there, while some banned them outright. This also capped the unmitigated growth in the scooter market. If scooters were not available when and where people needed them because cities limited their number or location, then this had a negative effect on how much upside there was on revenue.

Another thing that drives unit economics is the differentiation that you're able to build for your brand, product, or service over time. One of the ways to influence unit economics is your ability to change prices, based on the value that you're providing. Usually this differentiation is built into the barriers to entry because you have something unique that others cannot offer. That was not the case with scooters.

Most of the companies in the space were buying their scooters from Ninebot, which meant that almost anyone could start a own scooter business by simply buying Ninebot scooters, equipping them with the required GPS and ride-sharing equipment, and making an app available to the public. That's why in the early days so many scooter companies looked the same when we reviewed them. There were no barriers to entry, which was concerning to us as investors. There was no real customer loyalty. The switching costs came down to what scooter was immediately available when someone wanted to take a ride. The user experience was the same—download the app, unlock the scooter, and go for a ride. You could pay per ride or buy a subscription.

The experience that the customer got from each of these scooter-sharing companies was identical. The companies could paint their scooters different colors—black, yellow, orange, green—but that was about it. Ching-Yu Hu researched, spoke with, and closely examined the scooter-sharing market and many of the companies in it. She said:

> They were all using literally the same scooter. It was Ninebot, and they just put different stickers on it. Eventually, they tried to create their own vehicles, and maybe they had a little bit different battery life, but ultimately they were the same. It turns out when you have two companies with roughly the same offer, users have no brand loyalty. Their choice is the closest scooter to them. Therefore, these companies try to put as many scooters as possible out there, but they're capped by the cities, so then it creates this really odd dynamic of no competitive differentiation and therefore no opportunity to change unit economics. That's the rub.

Since there was no difference creation in the industry, the companies had no power to price their product at a profit. The companies constantly undercut each other's prices, turning scooters into a commodity. They were left to try to differentiate on cost.

When you break down the unit economics in terms of what are the cost levers, the revenue levers, and the differentiation levers that you're able to use, nothing was working in the industry's favor. All of these factors fundamentally doomed the scooter market. Investor capital can fund a lot of experimentation and user growth, but the underlying math of what it costs to deliver a product or service versus what a customer pays must make sense. The business model has to work not only in the short term, but also in the long term. If it doesn't, then failure will be the inevitable outcome.

Why didn't Next47 jump into this fast-growing market with both feet? When we looked at the business model—and more specifically, at the unit economics of the micromobility market—we didn't see a path to sustainable unit economics and profitability.

So much money was going in. There was unprecedented adoption. There seemed to be a lot of market demand. The companies built a product that served a need, causing this unprecedented adoption. These were all strong signals to invest. But when we looked more closely, we had a nagging concern. It all looked too good to be true. We made the decision not to invest in any company in that space, and the situation quickly turned sour. Each one of these scooter companies was burning cash at an unsustainable rate and growing everywhere—domestically and internationally. Ching-Yu explained:

> Over the last year, the market has consolidated heavily, and many of the operators have turned over their management. When COVID hit, these companies ended up saving money because they burned so much money running these operations—we found this a telling sign of how difficult it was to build an enduring business in micromobility. While we found the entrepreneurs in this space incredibly inspiring as they managed through explosive hypergrowth, we have no regrets not making a bet in this space in 2018.

The entire scooter economy crashed. Most of these companies essentially went from being unprecedented potential success stories to absolutely fighting for survival. If you look at 2020 in the post-COVID era, all of these companies are shadows of themselves.

A BUSINESS MODEL IS LIKE GRAVITY

Fundamentally, the absence of a profitable transaction between the parties will doom anything, even when you get a lot of other signals and hype. You start with a hypothesis for your business, usually "There's a customer problem, and there's a product that solves that problem." However, before you jump into serving the customers with your product, you must verify that there is a sustainable business model. So you verify and test your business model hypotheses and iterate through it.

By taking these steps, you can avoid business model failure—saving you a tremendous amount of time, money, and failures down the line when it's much more expensive and harder to fix. For example, when you hire two hundred people to build a product, send two hundred salespeople into the world to sell the product, and then are forced to change direction completely when you suddenly discover that customers won't pay for it, that's extremely expensive compared with getting the business model right from the outset.

Although the blue ocean strategy doesn't talk about unit economics, it does speak to the potential viability of a business model. Blue ocean emphasizes that you need to go into places that have no competition. When you move into a large, uncontested market space, it's amazing what a business can accomplish. In its early years, micromobility was a vast blue ocean, and the market really responded.

But the flip side of the blue ocean—and fundamentally every business—is that there has to be a long-term grounding and pathway to success. In the short term, you will get people to experiment and find growth because when there's usage, people want to find if there is a business. You'd better figure out quickly what your revenue levers, costs levers, and differentiation levers are. Just as quickly, you must find a way on a per-transaction or collection-of-transactions basis to convince yourself that it's actually going to make money in the long run and become sustainable.

If you don't get there, the fall can be as steep as the rise. Unit economics is like gravity. Whether we're talking about living on the planet Earth or building a business, at the end of the day, the law of gravity always applies.

COACHING THROUGH BUSINESS MODEL FAILURE

Once you have found your customer, your product, and a match between the two, you'll likely be excited about your business opportunity. Make no mistake about it: getting to this point is a real accomplishment. But once you've made it to this point, your business-building journey is not complete until you create a sustainable business model. This must be your focus.

Initially, it may or may not be clear what the business model is, and that's OK. In the initial period of uncertainty around the business, you need to have a hypothesis. The scooter-sharing companies had a hypothesis. Where they got ahead of themselves was in not fully pressure testing the hypothesis.

When you consider unit economics, you have three levers to work with: revenue, costs, and differentiation. Revenue and costs give you a snapshot of your financial position, while differentiation gives you a sense of sustainability. If you're able to make profits early on, but you don't have loyalty or barriers, you're going to lose the business because other entrants will dilute your economics as they compete for market share.

Your job as you build your business is to consider each of these three levers. What are the sources of revenue? What are the sources of costs? What are the sources of differentiation? Then put all of these things together and see if your hypothesis holds on the unit economics. If it holds, then you have something in your hand. If it doesn't hold, spending a lot of money is not going to get you where you want to go. You're not going to make it up in volume.

From a revenue perspective, it's important to understand what would cap your upside. You might, for example, find some early adopters, but are you going to find enough mainstream adopters to keep that growth going?

Is it possible you'll encounter unanticipated interventions from regulatory agencies or have problems with cybersecurity or privacy? Those are unintended interventions into revenue growth, and you have to look into things with the potential for this kind of impact. You also have to keep making sure that you're delivering enough value to reach an increasing number of customers.

From a cost perspective, you want to get into all the costs of your product or service, not just one piece of it. What is your cost of customer acquisition? What is your cost of actually delivering that product or service on an ongoing basis and not just one particular transaction? Are there going to be any third-party interventions, such as the theft and abuse that the scooter-sharing companies encountered? Will you need to share your economics with partners, and what are the costs of doing so?

Finally, from a differentiation perspective, why are you different, and how can you sustain this kind of profitable cycle of transacting? What are the barriers to entry, and do they make it difficult or easy for other people to enter? Is there customer loyalty? When you serve these customers, is there a reason for them to keep coming back to you? Are you doing something in terms of a way to transact with the customer that's compelling for them? Are there switching costs once a customer adopts your product?

Ultimately, differentiation and customer loyalty matter a lot to unit economics. When I think about a company that has an enviable combination of customer loyalty, barriers to entry, and a customer-friendly transaction model, I'm reminded of Netflix. In the early days, people hated Blockbuster, and they loved Netflix. They built customer loyalty because they didn't annoy their customers, but rather gave great service. Even though it was not instant gratification, people wanted to go and transact again. They were willing to wait to get that DVD in the mail.

Similarly, instead of paying on a per rental basis, Netflix offered a way to transact where you didn't have to think about it. They offered flat-fee subscriptions, and you could take as many DVDs as you wanted. They reduced this decision-making on a disc-by-disc basis into a set-it-once-and-forget-it type of thing. It was frictionless for customers.

One other thing was really important and different from Blockbuster: There were no charges for late fees. You could keep a DVD as long as you liked and return it whenever you wanted. At Blockbuster, if you were one minute late turning in your DVD, you were charged a late fee. In fact, in 2000, Blockbuster reported that it collected $800 million in late fees, which equated to 16 percent of the company's revenue for the year.[100] This was a major pain point for Blockbuster customers and a major source of loyalty for Netflix.

In terms of differentiation, you really have to innovate or have conviction that there are barriers to entry, and you can influence customer loyalty because you're doing something right. When you adopt a frictionless transaction model, this makes it easy for customers to stay and enjoy your service.

If there are thirty copycats, then that should tell you something about the barriers of entry. When your drivers have both Uber and Lyft emblems on their car dashboard, it tells you that neither the drivers nor the customers care which brand they choose. They simply want a car, and there's no customer loyalty.

In terms of making things frictionless, if everybody is doing the same thing, and you have nothing compelling like Netflix, then you're not differentiated on that dimension either. If there's no differentiation, this is not a good sign for the sustainability of your unit economics.

Remember: You can't defy the laws of gravity. You have to have a hypothesis. You need to break down your business model and unit economics to costs, revenue, and differentiation, and think through each category.

CHAPTER EIGHT

EXECUTION FAILURE

Since the beginning, delighting customers has been a central tenet of Amazon's culture. During the 2013 holiday season, UPS was overwhelmed with an unprecedented and unexpected volume of packages from Amazon and other online retailers. As a result, many Amazon packages scheduled to be delivered in time for Christmas Day gift giving were not, leading to numerous customer complaints. When all those packages arrived late, Amazon's customers were not delighted.

Amazon is obsessed with its customers and is wired to do everything in its power to create and maintain customer delight. This is what founder and then-CEO Jeff Bezos said in 1999 about the fear that drives the company's obsession with pleasing its customers:

I tell everybody at Amazon.com to wake up every morning absolutely terrified, drenching in sweat, but that they should be afraid of something very precise. They should be afraid of customers, not of competitors. And the reason is that it's the customers we have a relationship with. Our customers are loyal to us right up until the second that somebody else offers them a better service.

Amazon faced execution failure on Christmas Day 2013, and as a consequence their customers were deeply disappointed. Their leadership vowed it would never happen again. They realized that the only way to prevent a repeat fiasco would be to build their own delivery network, and they quickly set about doing just that.

When they began this new initiative, it seemed foolhardy for an online retailer—even one as large as Amazon—to replicate what UPS, FedEx, and DHL had spent decades creating and were already dominating.

By 2020, Amazon had become the fourth-largest U.S. delivery service, delivering more than half of its own packages to customers.[101] It's estimated that Amazon handled 5.1 billion packages in the United States in 2020, close to the 5.3 billion packages handled by UPS the same year.[102] It's expected that Amazon will pass up both UPS and FedEx within a few years as it continues to invest heavily in expanding its transportation operations, including delivery trucks and even aircraft. In 2020, the company added twelve Boeing 767-300s to its Amazon Air cargo fleet, bringing it to more than 80 aircraft.[103]

How did they do that? They turned execution failure into one of the most amazing feats ever of execution at scale.

They needed to compete, they set the goal, and they executed. And they accomplished all this in just a few years—that's *transformational* execution. That's the reason why people fear Amazon and why Amazon is worth so much.

PRIMACY OF EXECUTION

In any kind of business-building endeavor, once you have identified a customer need, figured out the technology, and decided on a product, and once you have your timing right, the right team in place, and a profitable business model, then success is virtually assured, right?

Not necessarily.

Whether you're a startup or an established incumbent, you need one more thing to win the race: *execution*. At the beginning of the race, victory is not preordained. In fact, at the beginning of the race, the incumbent usually has the advantage—their profit pools, technology capabilities, and strategy and motivation to compete.

What the startup brings to the table is fresh insight into how a market can be served, some capabilities to build a compelling product, and the ability to make and implement decisions much more quickly than the incumbent. However, it's execution that makes the difference and decides who will win and who will lose, which is why it demands your focus.

One of Next47's investments is a case in point on why execution matters above all.

VERKADA: EXECUTION IN A STARTUP CONTEXT

Verkada, a provider of cloud-based consumer and enterprise security solutions, is one of Next47's most successful portfolio companies. Since its founding in 2016, the company has grown by leaps and bounds—from thirty-eight customers in 2017 to more than fifty-five hundred in 2020, with a valuation in 2020 of $1.6 billion.[104] The founders' success is in great part due to their ability to execute.

Verkada's initial idea in creating the company was to say, "Hey, the consumer experience for owning a camera or having a thermostat in your house is so compelling, but when you dig into the world of physical security and how smart buildings are managed, you find a world of vendors that are really extremely old school. The technology stack for it had not been reinvented in years."

The founders saw the large market opportunity and the lack of innovation on the part of the incumbents. In addition, they had a vision for the pain point and how they could build a cloud-based product that would reduce the amount of on-premises complexity. Verkada created their initial product, and Next47 led their Series A investment. I joined the board at that time, and this gave me a compelling view on how the organization was run. I had a lot of confidence in the founding team because I had already seen executive chairman Hans Robertson operate and execute when he was at Meraki, and I could see that it was in CEO Filip Kaliszan's DNA to focus on what to do and getting it done.

Regardless, a lot of other name-brand investors were worried about all the incumbents in the space. Couldn't they do this, too? Would the old-school customers that dominated the market have a reason to adopt this new technology? How will you reach these customers? And what is your competitive advantage? There's no moat, and anyone can connect a camera to the cloud—Nest already has it. Why wouldn't Google go after this market? Some of the investors were afraid because the business was built around both hardware and software. They preferred pure software plays. However, Verkada's founders had a strong conviction that a pure software solution would not solve the customer's problem.

We saw an opportunity in Verkada's execution DNA and their ability to change and redefine the market, which was the starting point. The company executed—building compelling products—and some investors who previously were doubters came in and invested behind us. Today Verkada is doing well. They showed that if you can execute, you don't need some sort of magical advantage over the competition: Relentless execution is key to success.

In 2007, while he was studying computer science at Stanford, Filip Kaliszan started his first company, CourseRank, which was a class project turned into a business. He and the other founders saw the problem that they faced signing up for classes using Stanford's huge, printed class directories. Filip wondered why Stanford, in the heart of Silicon Valley, was still using paper directories when Amazon was making it easy to shop for products online. He and his co-founders built an online product that would make it easy for students to read about classes and then select and organize them. The company was acquired by Chegg in 2010, and Filip stayed on for several years to further develop the CourseRank product.

When Filip Kaliszan got together with Ben Bercovitz, James Ren, and Hans Robertson to found Verkada in 2016, they had two fundamental requirements for the company they would build. First, they wanted to start up a technology company where they would build something that was *cool*—a product that would keep them interested and engaged. Second, they wanted the market they were building a company in to be big and meaningful—one where they could make an impact. They gave themselves time to explore these two requirements of their startup before they went all in. Filip said:

> One of the best things we did that contributed to Verkada's success was we told ourselves that we would take a period of up to 12 months to explore different ideas without starting a company. But we worked very hard every day to build things and prototype them until we found an idea that met those two requirements that we felt good about that we wanted to chase.

About six months into the process, they settled on the idea of video security. Over the next six months, the team started prototyping products.

Driving the team forward was the question, "Do we have a shot at building something that is as awesome as something that Google or Apple built?" Verkada obviously couldn't build everything that Google and Apple did because those companies have giant teams and massive resources. But if Verkada could identify one or two experiences where they could do a better job then that would put them in a good position. Their first product wasn't perfect, but the team showed it could execute, iterate quickly, learn, and quickly improve. Filip explained:

Our first-ever product was missing many features. There is a saying that it's good to be embarrassed when you launch your first product. I wasn't just embarrassed, however; I was terrified. But there were a few aspects of this product that we got very excited about making better than what anyone else was doing. And those little touches made our product win. Any of our competitors could have done them, but they didn't. We did them, and we did them to a very high level of execution. And that's what got customers excited.

When we were considering investing in Verkada, I knew the space from my previous experience, and I was comfortable with this hardware/software type of hybrid model. Also, I knew it was a big category: No one needed to give me market sizing numbers to know this is a big category. I knew the products and the selling motions were all doable. It gets down to identifying the person who has the feel with the product and the willingness to build something amazing. I bought a camera and installed it in the office so I could try it for myself. It didn't have all the bells and whistles, but it had some compelling features, and it was easy to install and use.

In addition, I was looking for a team that could execute and was confident and independent and that wasn't going to call me every day for guidance. When I visited Verkada's offices, I could see that the boxes of cameras that people were buying were stacking up. They were actually making something, and they were selling it—they were *executing*. Filip said that the ability for any company to execute well starts with hiring the right people:

I've probably interviewed thousands of people at this point in this company, which is crazy. But one thing that was important for me from the very beginning—and

I'm trying to make it not just true for me, but for other teams in the company—is that everyone who reports to me that I hire is in some fashion better than me. I'm not interested in ever hiring someone who is less smart than me in a certain area. If I interview a product person, and I'm thinking, "I can do your job better than you think you can," then I know that's not the right person for the job.

During the next year, Verkada plans to more than double the size of its team. When you grow so quickly, you're bound to make mistakes and Verkada is no exception. The company has hit some bumps in the road. When this team encounters a challenge though, they lean on their execution prowess to learn, course correct, and make good decisions that keep them on the path to success.

To succeed in the long run, you need people who can identify mistakes, take corrective action, and never repeat those mistakes. You need high performers to really move the needle. If someone isn't executing, then it's really important to act on it quickly. How you handle these kinds of decisions will dictate a significant portion of the overall team's ability to execute and ultimately their performance.

Decision-making goes to the heart of execution—the faster and better you make key decisions, the faster and better your company can execute. In Filip's experience, there are two kinds of problems that any decision-maker must deal with: problems that are urgent but not important and problems that are important. It's critical that decision-makers can identify and separate the two, and act upon them appropriately. If you don't, then you will be overwhelmed, dealing with the problems that are urgent but not important. Filip explained:

It's important for every executive to dedicate their time where it really matters most. And in my case, it's focusing on the things that are important, not urgent.[105] I have hired people in different areas that I think of as better than me—people I can trust and delegate a lot of the urgent problems to. That frees me up to focus my time and energy on the things that make the greatest difference over the company's long term.

The most basic example of this for us is probably long-term product execution versus near-term sales execution. Certainly, if I was in every deal call, I think we could move the needle by maybe 20, 30, or maybe even 40 percent the next two quarters. And is that urgent? Sure, that's urgent because many of our investors would get excited if we made more money tomorrow. But is that where I should focus my time? I don't think so.

What I put in the category of being important—the kind of problem I should focus on is thinking about how to build a product that we will launch 6 or 12 or 18 months from now, and how that product integrates with everything else. I could spend the same amount of time making an incremental increase in sales—say $10 million in the next quarter—or on the new product. But if I focus my time on the new product, I might actually create the kernel or foundation of something that becomes billions of dollars of market opportunity or value over the long term. That's where I need to focus my time, and that's where I personally execute.

However, when someone on the team comes to Filip to get his opinion, he doesn't shy away from giving it. He has hired a team that he respects and that can make decisions without him for the most part, which frees up time for him to focus on the important things that need his attention and makes the company more resilient. But when he is asked for his opinion, that opens up communication—keeping the team more closely aligned and cohesive in their thinking and building confidence to execute independently and quickly, knowing that they're all on the same page.

I have nothing but deep admiration for Filip, Hans, and the entire team at Verkada, and their ability to execute with passion and precision every day. Execution has put Verkada on a trajectory to be a category leader in physical security for a long time.

SIEMENS: EXECUTION IN A LARGE, TURNAROUND CONTEXT

While much emphasis is put on execution in a startup setting, where growing quickly and gaining market share can make or break you, I believe it is just as important for large enterprises in mature markets.

Dr. Roland Busch is currently the president and CEO of Siemens AG, a diversified multinational company that offers products and services in everything from industrial automation and digitalization to smart infrastructure, mobility, and diagnostic and therapeutic imaging. From its founding by Werner von Siemens in 1847, the company has grown into a global powerhouse with annual revenues of more than €57 billion in 2020.[106] Roland has been with Siemens for more than twenty-five years, starting as a researcher and working his way up through executive leadership positions in a variety of business units, from

Infotainment Solutions to Siemens VDO Automotive to Mass Transit and eventually membership on the company's managing board.

In 2008, Roland became head of Corporate Strategy for Siemens. During his three years in that position, he and his team focused on what to do with the Siemens portfolio of businesses. At the time, Siemens had three major sectors: Industry, Healthcare, and Energy. The Industry sector was huge, with many unrelated business units under its umbrella. The strategy team thought it would be a good idea to break out a fourth sector from the Industry and Energy sectors and to give it a theme. This new sector became Infrastructure and Cities, and it contained such things as mobility with rolling stock (trains), logistics, building technology, medium- and low-voltage electrical grid, and more. Roland joined the managing board and was put in charge of this new business sector.

However, when Siemens formed this sector, the German press wasn't too kind, calling it *Reste sind hier* or "leftovers are here." The original three sectors—Energy, Healthcare, and Industry— had at least one eight hundred-pound gorilla that anchored each sector. This was a big business, number one in their market, that produced so much cash and profit that a bad business could be easily hidden behind it. At Siemens, as in many large enterprises, they sometimes were so hidden.

The mobility business was not very profitable when Roland took over, and a couple of months later, he recognized that there was a big problem in the rolling stock business. They kept making promises to deliver on a high-speed train project, but they were unable to follow through. They set up a meeting with the then-CEO of Siemens, the CEO of Deutsche Bahn, and Roland —again promising that they would deliver by a specific date.

But two weeks later, on the promised date, they did not.

The Siemens managing board was not happy, and they expected Roland to turn around this €18 billion business—not in a year or two, but in two or three quarters. His first job was helping the managing board understand that turning around such a large business would take time. Sure, he could have agreed to squeeze the organization and deliver better results more quickly, but they would not be sustainable since they were at surface level and weren't the result of real change within the organization. Achieving lasting results requires going below the surface and creating real substance. Roland explained:

> I said to my people, "I won't claim victory until you deliver at least eight quarters in a row of really making your numbers. Not necessarily top of the margin, but you make your numbers, and you climb the ladder." Motivating my team was a real challenge at the time. They read the newspapers, which called them the "leftovers," they were the underdogs, they weren't making their margins, they weren't making their incentives, and they were always at the end of the line. When we had management presentations, the highest-performing groups were always at the beginning and the worst ones at the end. The rolling stock business always presented at the end. How motivating is that?

After explaining to Siemens's managing board that turning around the train business would take more than a few quarters, Roland's next question was this: How do you get these people motivated? The first thing he did was to create a reasonable and acceptable budget that was achievable. "My point was, even if you are not on par with your competitors or your basket, you have to make a budget where you start making your numbers." Then, when the team executes, delivers, and makes the numbers, create a new budget that raises the bar a bit higher.

As the team continues to execute and deliver, this raises their confidence and morale along with creating the momentum necessary for the team to achieve good outcomes continuously. People on the team begin to say, "We are not that bad. We are delivering according to our yardstick." And indeed they were, consistently.

Roland also realized that it was important to create an identity for the new sector. It turned out that Infrastructure and Cities—particularly the *cities* element—made people stand up and pay attention. They recognized that cities were the place where everybody had something in common. They're *living* in cities. And if they could help make cities better, then that was something to identify with and be proud of. Regardless of which business unit they were working for—mobility, buildings, low- or medium-voltage—they all said, "We are working for Infrastructure and Cities." And as they made their numbers and gained momentum, they said, "OK, we stick together as we are the underdogs, and we're going to make it together."

According to Roland, the change in attitude within the team was palpable:

> *During our first management meeting, everyone was curious, insecure: "What's happening to me? Now I'm part of this leftovers group!" The second management meeting was when we really hit our low because we*

didn't deliver, we screwed it up. But then by the third meeting, the mood began to turn positive—we had by then delivered on one or two targets. And at the fourth one, people were really celebrating because we felt we were in control. We were turning something around, and we had created momentum.

However, there was more to turning around this business than setting achievable budgets and creating an identity that employees could identify with and embrace. As an executive or manager in charge of turning around a business, you've got to dig through the different layers of bureaucracy to see what's really going on. Only then can you fix it.

The day after the rolling stock business unit missed the delivery deadline they had promised the CEOs of Siemens and Deutsche Bahn, Roland booked a trip to the headquarters of the mobility business where they were engineering and manufacturing the train. He called a meeting of the management team—the division, business unit, and segment managers—and said to them, "You set me up because you said go there, and we promised that we would deliver, and we didn't. I want to understand why."

Their response in the meeting was to start a presentation with pretty photos. "This is the train, and this is the order," they said.

"No, no" Roland quickly responded. "You don't get me. I want to understand why we didn't get the acceptance. What is the problem?"

"What do you mean?" the managers asked, confused by Roland's unexpected interest in the details of the business unit's failure.

"Tell me the failures that prevented the homologation and delivery of the train," Roland said. The managers had set up the meeting with him and the two CEOs not even knowing with any degree of certainty that they would be able to deliver as they promised.

"Yes, but there are *many* failures," responded the managers.

"Fine," Roland told them. "I want you to go through them one, by one, by one."

"But we have not prepared a presentation for it," they replied, no doubt hoping that Roland would accept their excuse and move on.

"I don't care," Roland pressed. "I will digest anything. Bring me your Excel spreadsheet, whatever you have—your failure document."

"Oh, we don't have it," was the response. "Maybe we will have to call for the project manager."

"Then call for the project manager," Roland suggested. "I'm sitting here, and we'll run through them one, by one, by one."

He continued:

> We ended up running through 62 failures, one after the other—in software, in hardware, in everything. And I wanted to understand the reasons why: one, by one, by one. They couldn't understand what the whole thing was about. The project manager was unable to explain all of the failures, and neither could the segment manager, the business unit manager, nor the division head. There were basically four levels of hierarchy, and none of them was deep enough to understand what the problem was on this project with a €300 million impact. And it's not like the problems had just started yesterday—they had been building for more than five years. For me, this was completely unacceptable.

Roland told the managers that he expected them to have a great depth of knowledge of their product, not in every case, but where the project was big enough or critical enough to pull down their division. "I want you to know what's going on," he said.

And because their boss began to hold them accountable, they started to make a point of knowing what was going on, and they started executing at a higher level.

The next time Roland called a meeting of the rolling stock management team, he told them he wanted to work through the failures again, one by one by one. The managers were ready this time, and when he asked a question like, "Why is failure number 14 not on your list anymore?" they could give a good answer. They knew he was serious. And from that time forward, Roland could call his business unit or division manager on any project, and they knew what was going on. They knew what the expectation was, and they delivered.

Said Roland, "I will personally dive as deep as necessary, even as a board member, if something is going wrong. And I expect each line manager below to do the same, full stop, very simple. It works."

This is not a one hundred thousand-foot approach to managing a business. Instead, it really gets down to the operational details and making sure those things flow smoothly. The result is that the train business is now one of the most consistent businesses in Siemens. It has been profitable for more than five years, quarter over quarter.

Roland inculcated the idea of operational discipline and execution into the train business along with getting down to the matters that were actually getting in the way and moving on them. It was not about some massive blinding insight on how to fix these underperforming businesses. It was not Michael Porter's approach to strategy; it was not blue ocean; it wasn't any of those things. It was just plain old-fashioned elbow grease, discipline, and execution.

After sparking the turnaround of the train business, Roland turned his attention to the low-voltage business. Before it was moved into the new Infrastructure and Cities sector, Siemens's low-voltage business was sitting next to an eight hundred-pound gorilla—Automation. And guess who got the money to grow the business? The eight hundred-pound gorilla. While the automation people were sitting in offices, there wasn't enough space for the low-voltage employees, so they were put in cubicles.

The low-voltage business had a portfolio of molded case circuit breakers (MCCBs), which for many years didn't get the investment needed to grow. When the low-voltage business was brought into Infrastructure and Cities, Roland first committed to getting them the investment they needed, but with the caveat that they step up their execution. They would need to sequence their product rollouts—deciding on the first product to launch, and then the second, and so on. Then Roland built the low-voltage business a new building that cost several million euros and would get them out of the cubicles and into real offices.

Next Roland turned his attention to the go-to-market. He discovered that when the low-voltage sales team was sitting under the umbrella of the automation gorilla, they mostly sold automation instead of low-voltage products. If customers wanted a low-voltage product, they had to ask for it. This was not how you sell your low-voltage products. Roland also figured out that the salesforce was mostly selling to industry customers, which was only about 20 percent of the low-voltage market. The other

80 percent of the market was construction, buildings, and infrastructure, which was an entirely different channel. This was very material in China which was the biggest market of all.

The head of Infrastructure and Cities for China told Roland, "This is not going anywhere because you're still relying on the existing salesforce." And it was true: They had relied on the existing salesforce, and they weren't focused on selling the low-voltage products. So Roland decided it was time for low-voltage to have its own sales team. The existing team could still sell low-voltage products if they liked, but if low-voltage was going to start really executing in China, they needed their own dedicated sales team—even if that meant spending whatever it took to set it up. Roland explained what happened next:

> The low-voltage business was growing by 7 percent before, which in China is below market. Normally, you should grow by, say, 9 to 10 percent. In the first quarter, the head of the new low-voltage sales team was really very quick in hiring people, and we had some people selling into the construction market who really pushed it hard. Quarter, by quarter, by quarter, this business grew between 20 and 25 percent. It was literally like switching on a light because we had been disregarding 80 percent of the market. And you have to understand that Siemens in China is an extremely strong brand. When customers saw the Siemens brand on our products, they knew they were buying the highest quality.

In addition to creating a dedicated salesforce for low-voltage, Roland put a manager in charge and allowed him to run the organization without interference. The manager changed the incentive scheme for salespeople, enabling them to earn as much as they could. But people who went two quarters without meeting their targets were out. He constantly added new salespeople to the team—rewarding those who executed and removing those who did not. He knew exactly which strings to pull to get the people in this organization to perform, and they did. Roland said:

> At the end of the day, it's about the people and how you get, in a positive sense, the most out of them. This starts with picking the right people to do the right things. Someone who is very good at strategy or vision might not be so good at execution. Someone who is a great turnaround manager might not be great at running a business that is already running well—they will screw it up. Something else that is important is a person's values. If the values are not straight, normally you can figure that out in the first four weeks. And don't believe that this is going to change in the next three years. If there's a misfit in values, you'd better act fast.

> We try to have a growth mindset at Siemens, which is ultimately about openness. Very often, people are not open for accepting their failures or problems. However, if you're not open to that, then how can you improve? I believe you cannot.

As Roland clearly understands, you don't get the best performance out of an organization by creating obstacles to the success of your people and then punishing them when they can't execute. You don't hang a sign on the wall that says, "The beatings will continue until morale improves." Instead, you remove these obstacles in every way you can, then put everyone on the team in a position where they can best utilize their natural talents to be successful. In the case of the low-voltage business, this meant creating an entirely new sales organization focused on selling those particular products, with salespeople incentivized and motivated to do just that.

According to Roland, there are two core elements of being an effective manager, and both go to the heart of execution: discipline and persistence. When you have discipline, you can keep your focus on the task at hand—avoiding distractions that impede progress toward your goal. And when you have persistence, you will try and try again until you nail whatever it may be that you are working to accomplish.

This combination of discipline and persistence enables you to execute and create real substance for your business, value for your customers, and return for your shareholders.

COACHING THROUGH EXECUTION FAILURE

To exaggerate for effect, a business's success is 1 percent based on getting the things we talked about in the previous chapters right—the customer, the technology, the product, the team, the timing, and the business model—and 99 percent based on getting the execution right.

There's a quote that rings true for me that has been attributed to everyone from Thomas Edison to Henry Ford, Albert Einstein, and even America Online founder Steve Case. Regardless of who first said the words, they are remarkably insightful:

A vision without execution is just a hallucination.

You can create something that customers really need and love, but without execution on consistently getting the product in the hands of all the customers who need it, you have nothing.

You can have the greatest technology in the world, but without execution on removing the barriers to adoption, you have nothing.

You can have the best product ever, but without execution on changing customer outcomes and improving rapidly, you have nothing.

You can have a remarkable team, but without execution on matching talent to priorities, building the right culture, and motivating everyone to be at their very best, you have nothing.

You can have perfect timing, but without execution on competing and winning on the ground, you have nothing.

And you can have a profitable business model, but without execution that generates profits in the real world, you have nothing.

After you anticipate and address all the potential sources of failure detailed in the preceding chapters and get everything right, you've still got to execute. It's easy to come up with excuses—the product is missing features, the team isn't delivering, the dog ate the homework—but excuses get you nowhere. Focus on the fundamentals: If something's not working, fix it. And execute, day after day after day. There's no substitute for focus and execution.

FOUR ASPECTS OF EXECUTION

When we say "execution," what are we really talking about? How do you avoid execution failure? In my experience, there are four key ways that companies execute: focus, speed, relentlessness, and decision-making.

Focus is having clarity on what to do and what not to do and sticking with it. This requires having principles or criteria by which you are clear on what you're going to do and what you're not going to do. As an upstart, you don't have infinite resources, and you don't have forever to get it right. Therefore, you have to be clear on what you're going to apply your resources against and why. That focus on what to do and what not to do has to permeate everything that you do as you run the race. Saying "no" to many, many things so that you can say "yes" to what matters is the essence of focus.

Speed is moving quickly and with greater agility than the competition. If you can be faster in building the product, responding to what the customers want, building out a go-to-market that's fit for purpose with the market opportunity, listening to customers, and incorporating their feedback in what you do, then that will differentiate you from everyone else.

Relentlessness is the idea that you're fighting the fight every day, over and over, and getting the details right—big and small. That kind of relentlessness also allows you to win segments of a large opportunity. Yes, you can serve three hundred million people, but before you can serve that many, you've first got to serve thirty people, and then thirty thousand people, and then three hundred thousand people, and so on. Every time you get knocked down, you get up and go at it again.

Decision-making is, of course, making choices between one course of action and another. In general, many people get the large decisions right. We need to do this and this against an opportunity. But then it breaks down into a number of what I call *micro decisions* across the organization and getting a majority of them right. That's really the crux of what great execution is about. You can say, "OK, we want to be in this market, and we want to launch this product, and we want to compete." Then you've got to make all the micro decisions to achieve your goals: who to hire and who not to hire, which product features to focus on first to drive your initial traction versus which features to offer later, which customers to serve and which customers not to serve, or how to react to feedback and make adjustments to your hypothesis. There are hundreds of micro decisions to be made, and to execute and move the business forward, you need to get them right most of the time.

DAVID VERSUS GOLIATH

One of the reasons that people fear companies like Apple, Amazon, and Microsoft is that they are Goliaths that can execute. You don't want to take them on—you can't *afford* to take them on. Not only are these Goliaths deeply entrenched in their markets, with essentially unlimited resources, but they've proven time and again that they can execute—and execute *precisely*—against new opportunities and potential disruptions.

And what about the Goliaths that once dominated their respective markets—companies such as Eastman Kodak, Blockbuster, and Toys R Us? Why did they fail? I believe it's because they lost their way when it came to applying the full strength of their execution capabilities against the disruptive threats. As Clay Christensen suggests in his book *The Innovator's Dilemma*, these incumbent Goliaths continued to execute on the things that made them successful—their core business—while disruptive new technologies, products, platforms, and ecosystems grew rapidly all around them. This gave the upstart Davids the opening they were looking for, and they didn't hesitate to take it.

Consider the example of Amazon, the onetime David that made many long-established brick-and-mortar Goliaths such Toys R Us, Borders, and Sears irrelevant. In 1997, Amazon built its first two fulfillment centers, in Seattle, Washington, and New Castle, Delaware, and it added a handful more in the ensuing years. However, with the 2005 introduction of Amazon Prime—the subscription service that promised unlimited two-day "free" shipping of purchases on the site—Amazon began a dramatic expansion from that handful of fulfillment centers to hundreds of them. In 2020 alone, Amazon added more than 220 new package facilities—from cavernous warehouses to small, urban delivery stations.[107] This is top-notch execution toward the goal to better serve customers while controlling costs.

In the technology business, stories of challengers outexecuting incumbents abound.

Oracle versus Sybase.

Intel versus Motorola.

Microsoft versus IBM.

Salesforce versus Siebel.

Each of these business pairings is a David-versus-Goliath story, where a younger, more agile company took on a long-entrenched, much larger competitor and won. At the starting point of the race, the companies that ultimately lost had technical superiority, market presence, resources, and a reasonable strategic framework to compete. The upstarts seemed to have insurmountable odds.

Yet the upstarts won. They executed against the opportunity in front of them. Execution is not glamorous, but it's exactly why David can beat Goliath despite the odds.

CHAPTER NINE

TRANSFORMING FAILURE INTO SUCCESS

Now that we have considered the many modes of failure when you are building a new business, how can this knowledge change your thought process and approach? You are armed with this toolkit—what can you do with it? How do you take the concepts you've read and put them into practice? While the search for a unified theory for business success continues among pundits and celebrities, my aspirations are more pragmatic. In this chapter, I share how to anticipate failure and navigate your path to success in a practical way.

In the real world, we have to remember that all narratives of success and failure are viewed in hindsight, and the picture for you in real time may be incomplete. The data points are not necessarily going to be clear, and you may have to make decisions before you have all the information at your fingertips. That's just the way it's going to be. The examples you encounter in your own business may not be as obvious as some of the ones we have discussed in this book, and that's OK.

Also keep in mind that there will *always* be exceptions. Some say, for example, that Steve Jobs never did customer discovery. That may or may not be true, but what is definitely the case is that Jobs always started with the customer in mind. And even so, he had many product failures—Apple Lisa, Power Mac G4 Cube, Macintosh TV, and others—in addition to tremendous successes such as the iPhone, iTunes store, and iPad.

My goal here is not to establish a unified theory of failure with no exceptions. Rather, it's to sensitize you to the main sources of failure and the importance of getting the basics right—such things as understanding your customers' pain points, having sound unit economics, building a team with purpose, and so on. You can exist in the failure zone for some time—longer if you have sufficient funds—and you can find your way out of it. To succeed, you *must* find your way out of it.

As you look to diagnose and deal with failure and set yourself up for success, here are some ways to craft your approach using the principles we covered in the earlier chapters. Again, these are not prescriptions for success. Instead, I consider them to be coaching reminders of how to navigate through failure and achieve success in real life. Imagine me calling them out to you as you advance down the field of play. (Dear non-sports-fans—sorry for the American football metaphor.)

SAME OPPORTUNITY, MANY LENSES

Let me begin with how we apply the anticipate failure mindset in the world of venture capital. We look at every opportunity through the many different lenses or failure modes we have explored together in the previous chapters. Naturally, there will be overlaps. When the opportunity is the same, but you look at it through different lenses, you might get different insights. The biggest reason to have these different lenses is to avoid blind spots.

When we are in a pitch meeting, many founders have the ability to bend reality. We may become enamored with one part of the narrative and one potential outcome. The reason we have these different lenses is to take that narrative and look at it from varied perspectives. Is the timing right? Is the product right? Is there a real customer need? Do they have the right founding team? Do the economics work out? Is there a proven track record that shows they can actually execute the plan they're talking about?

These different lenses allow us to holistically assess an opportunity, and that's what we're talking about here as well.

Each of us in venture capital has certain lenses that are our natural strengths. My personal focus is on the customer, timing, and the ability to execute. My partner at Next47, T. J. Rylander, has a focus on products and technology. And my second partner, Matthew Cowan, focuses on team strengths, unit economics, and the ability to position in a market and either create a new category or outcompete.

When checking or diagnosing failure, the key is not to take this on as a solo task, but instead to leverage the strengths of your team. Bring in a diverse group of people who will apply different lenses based on their strengths, then collectively come up with better decisions. This is the practice in the best venture firms, and it is effective.

THE JOURNEY OF 1,000 MILES BEGINS WITH ONE STEP

When you're in business-building mode, it's important to have a destination in mind, the vision for the destination, and the conviction that the journey is worthwhile. In every case, the failures that I detailed in the previous chapters were disappointing, but the destinations were absolutely worthwhile.

Ratan Tata's idea for the Nano automobile was to serve the underserved and give them a better quality of life. That was a worthwhile destination. Dean Kamen's idea for the Segway was to provide people with a convenient, space-saving mode of urban transportation without too many carbon emissions. That was a worthwhile destination. We all know the journey is going to be one thousand miles, but planning every single mile is simply not possible.

You'll have to take that first step and ask yourself a variety of questions: How am I going to put the initial team together? What's the minimum viable product going to look like? How am I going to get the first few customers? How am I going to get the first million of revenue? As you find answers for these questions, you must avoid the trap of trying to plan to perfection every step of the way for the next five years. That will slow you down, and in a hypercompetitive environment, you can't afford delay. You need to get started and then iterate as you learn more.

When you are acting and failing, at least you're learning. And when you learn, you have a chance to reposition yourself. But if you're stalled or stuck in place, then you're not learning, and you're not addressing the failure. No worthwhile endeavor is risk free, and when you are in the golden window of opportunity, not acting is a greater risk than acting, failing, and learning.

Whether you're building a business as a founder, or you're inside a large company, you have to begin that journey. You cannot be mired in thousands of decisions that will take forever, or try to get false fidelity of information that you don't have right now. You can speculate on a lot of things, and then you can try to build a huge plan to have your one thousand miles mapped out, but that plan inevitably will change when you hit your first challenge.

One of my favorite quotes is from heavyweight boxing champ Mike Tyson: "Everyone has a plan until they get punched in the mouth." The idea is you've got to take the first step, and you've got to enter the fray because the destination is worth it. You need to have your idea, but then you've got to be practical about getting started and not being frozen because you're worried that something might go wrong. Know that even the best-laid plans are going to change as you get more data. You've got to be agile and ready to alter course at a moment's notice. In my experience with companies, this is less advice for a typical founder, but more relevant for larger companies where people often allow fear to paralyze them.

EVERYTHING IS GREAT ALL THE TIME

When you're building your business, you've got to be intellectually honest. Acknowledging a failure mode is for your own benefit. The more honest you are in your assessment, the better off you're going to be in doing what needs to be done to anticipate failure and get through it. When we meet with younger venture capitalists and younger founders who haven't been through these things before, they'll usually say, "Everything in my portfolio is great—this company is amazing, everything about it is great."

But when you meet with more seasoned venture capitalists or founders who have been through the journey before, they express optimism but are cognizant of reality. Without optimism, nothing can be built. Without this vision for the future—how the world can be a better place—and a belief in your own abilities and progress so far, you can't succeed. Those are all essential, and that's optimism. But let's not confuse that with "Everything is great all the time." If you find yourself in the mode of managing perceptions and spending a lot of time *thinking* about how great everything is, then you're going down the wrong path, and you're not making an effort to avoid failure.

From the outside, it appears that this is what happened with Quibi. The destination was worthwhile, and they had a great team. But in hindsight, they seem to have had several problems that all the optimism in the world could not fix. I suspect a lot of "Everything is great all the time" was going on inside the company. No one wanted to give anyone bad news. They just kept saying, "This is great, this is great." And they just kept going until they hit a wall.

The same seemed to be the case with the Tata Nano. Perhaps because the product was the brainchild and vision of chairman Ratan Tata, the organization was not willing to take a good, hard look at what was going wrong and what they could fix. They weren't intellectually honest about the real market for the car—they were projecting contrary to reality, and that ultimately doomed Nano.

THE LACK OF SPEED KILLS

Next47 partner T. J. Rylander quips that a lack of speed kills in business building. There is so much truth to this. Speed is all about execution—the ability to take an idea, build a hypothesis around the idea as to what outcomes you're trying to achieve with it, take the action, see the results, and then build a feed-back loop. Chances are that you're embarking on a mission or a path that others have not tried before. It's essential to maxi-mize the speed of translating ideas into action, seeing results, getting feedback, and then feeding what you've learned into your hypotheses—making necessary changes along the way.

This applies to not only what you're doing in the business, but also when you're applying your different lenses to anticipate and detect failure. Once you detect failure, you need a plan for how you're going to address it and what you're going to do if you need to keep working at it because you may not get it done on the first try. That's why this idea of translating into action, seeing results, taking feedback, and doubling down on what works and what doesn't work is an important aspect.

If you look at the universe of successful startups, most have gone through these cycles. When I worked at Hewlett-Packard,

Meg Whitman once shared that in hindsight, she never felt that she had let someone go too early. It's always the case that you realize you let someone go too late. We want to give them the benefit of the doubt, or we believe them when they tell us that they'll turn things around, or we're just too busy putting out big fires to douse the smaller ones. Whatever the reason, when we hang onto someone who isn't helping the team accelerate, it's just slowing you down. If you see a problem with the team, and you don't act, then that lack of speed is going to kill you.

Meraki's good fortune was having a founding team with complementary strengths that filled in the gaps that each one of them could not bring on their own. Some organizations are not so fortunate, and as they grow, one or more members of the founding team may not be able to grow fast enough to keep up—endangering the long-term prospects of the organization. Convincing a founder to step down or step back in such a situation is a difficult, but sometimes necessary conversation to have.

The quality and reputation of Verkada's founding team attracted other high-quality talent, accelerating the company's growth. Make no mistake about it—not every new employee they hire turns out to be the right choice. Instead of allowing underperformers to stick around and potentially hire other low performers, they weed them out right away. It's tough at a personal level when someone has to leave, but acting fast and being fair is much better than dragging out the inevitable.

When Siemens built its first CT scanner, the product team quickly realized that doctors were not going to be happy for long with a machine that scanned only human heads, as amazing as that technology was at the time. They soon were going to want and need a full-body scanner. The Siemens team quickly progressed to where the future was going to be and were the first to market with the next step in CT, whole-body scanners, when customers were ready for it. Speed to what's next for the customer wins.

USE DATA TO UNDERSTAND, NOT JUSTIFY

Data is a powerful tool, and managing with data is an important aspect of business building. It's not managing through stories, but really managing through data. In my experience, you can either have a story and use the data to tell it, or you can really look at the data and let the story emerge organically from the roots. These two approaches have very different consequences.

The team that Gokul Rajaram worked with at Facebook decided to try something new: Create a lightweight product for page owners to create and run ad campaigns on the platform. Their hypothesis was that with this new feature, page owners would create and run more ad campaigns, increasing advertising revenue for Facebook. They created the feature, launched it, then stepped back to see what would happen. A few thousand page owners initially signed up, but most canceled their subscriptions within a month. The new feature was a flop.

The team could have taken the initial sign-up data to Gokul and said, "Hey, we're having some moderate success right out of the gate," and they could have used this data to tell a story about their product launch being a great success. Instead they said, "Hey, the product launch was not as great as we predicted it would be. Why was that?" I've seen the former behavior often, in startups as well as large companies. When the team is under pressure and under scrutiny, it's much easier for them to use the data to tell their story. It takes courage to stop doing that. And you must because it's going to harm you in the long run—your growth will be stunted.

You need to use the data, get down to what is actually happening, and truly make an effort. If you do that—as was the case with the Facebook team—you can achieve a great outcome. The Facebook team's initial hypothesis was wrong, and when they dug into why that was the case, they identified the problem: There was a mismatch between their offer and what customers wanted. The customers wanted to control their advertising, and the new feature took away that control. The team's mindset was that they would use data to understand, not to justify. In doing so, they experienced a small failure, but they got through it and gained an understanding of what their customer really wanted.

UNCONVENTIONAL WISDOM

In any business-building endeavor, you are, by definition, doing something bold and new. What that means is that on occasion, you have to change what is the accepted conventional wisdom and what everyone else thinks or expects you to do. Therefore, when you are making a decision, being clear-headed about it is important for your direction and destiny. If it really matters to your business, then take the time to think through first principles and what matters here, and don't be overly swayed by conventional wisdom. It's only by doing unconventional things that you can achieve truly great outcomes.

Consider the example of Meraki, where the conventional wisdom would have told them, "You're selling a networking product, so the smart thing to do is hire salespeople from the most dominant networking company, Cisco, or just sell your products through Cisco's channel partners." But when they started down that path, they quickly realized that it was not leading them to the outcomes they wanted.

Because of Cisco's dominance in the networking market, the company's salespeople were for the most part not able to hunt customers—they were order takers. If Meraki hired salespeople away from Cisco, they weren't getting the right kind of people— they weren't *hunters*. The second thing they realized was that Cisco channel partners were more or less captives to the company—their livelihoods depended on Cisco. So they had no incentive to carry or sell Meraki's products.

What did Meraki do? They looked for salespeople in highly competitive business product arenas such as copiers, which was a cutthroat market. Copier salespeople were hunters who were accustomed to fighting for every sale. Once Meraki started hiring this kind of salesperson, their revenues began to increase.

Instead of placing their products with Cisco channel partners, they targeted computer retailers—sellers of, for example, PCs and servers—that routinely carried multiple products and were not beholden to any one particular company. Meraki intentionally made their products so easy to use that even someone who didn't have a deep networking knowledge could sell it effectively. When they sold a new computer to a customer, they could upsell the Meraki networking product as a value-add. This extended the wallet for the channel partner, as opposed to going through a Cisco channel partner where their wallets would get hurt.

This kind of unconventional thinking was required, and Meraki had to break the conventional wisdom mold to achieve success.

Another example of bucking the conventional wisdom led Google to pioneer cloud computing. Google's first data center was a seven-by-four-foot cage that it put together in 1998 in the Exodus co-location space in Santa Clara, California. This first data center comprised thirty personal computers on shelves. Exodus also hosted data centers for eBay, Altavista, Inktomi, and many other dot-com elite companies at the time.[108] As Google caught on with users, and searches exploded, the company needed to add far more computing capability—and quickly. There was constant pressure on the company to deliver search results faster and better.

In 1999, when the number of machines on which Google ran had grown to 112, the company placed an order for 1,680 servers. But these weren't just any servers. At the time, the conventional wisdom was that a data center should be built on a foundation of powerful, sophisticated, bulky, and expensive Sun servers. Instead, Google's founders, Sergey Brin and Larry Page, decided that it would be more cost-effective to design their own servers, using cheap, off-the-shelf computer boards and other hardware.

Google placed the order for 21 server cabinets with local King Star Computer. Each cabinet contained 80 servers comprising a Supermicro motherboard with 265 megabytes of memory, an Intel Pentium II CPU, two IBM 22-gigabyte hard drives, and an Intel network card. These server cabinets were as bare-bones as they could be—four bare motherboards on a shelf with no cases—but they were powerful, flexible, and relatively inexpensive at a cost of $110,000 for each cabinet.[109] This unconventional approach allowed Google to scale up quickly as searches exploded. Expanding capacity just meant adding another server cabinet.

And when it came to software, the conventional wisdom was to buy and run Oracle's database and application server products, which were the gold standard at the time. But they were expensive, and they were proprietary, so Google wrote and ran their own code. Instead of buying expensive hard drives designed for long lifespans, they anticipated that the discs would fail, and they bought inexpensive but speedy hard drives meant for personal computers, not high-end servers. This kind of unconventional thinking eventually led them to become a pioneer in cloud computing.

But more important, they had their eye on the ball to say, "How do we make the cost of a search so insignificant that we can provide it as a free service to everyone? If only a small portion of what we do is monetized, then we can still build a fantastic business." If Google had followed the conventional wisdom and bought Sun servers, Oracle software, and expensive enterprise hard drives, they would have helped make those companies rich, but they would not have become the Google we know today.

DON'T BELIEVE IN MAGIC

When you embark on an expedition, let's say to the Antarctic or to the moon, each person on the team has to be amazing. They also must have special and complementary skills and roles. In business building, if you have something really worthwhile, you're going to need more than the effort of a lone genius or the founding team. You must have a lot of talented and hardworking people who will help you get to the worthwhile destination that you have set.

The idea is that your fellow travelers, who bring along their special skills and roles, are important in any expedition. Yes, you need an expedition leader, but you also need a navigator, and someone to handle logistics, and an engineer who can operate, maintain, and repair communications and other equipment. You need someone who will set up and pack tents, and someone who will cook meals. Everyone has a particular role, and some members of the team may take on more than one role.

All of the people on the expedition were hired because they are outstanding at what they do. If you as the leader say, "I'll just hire clones of myself," or "I'm going to hire only people who are willing to take my orders without questioning them," you won't just jeopardize the expedition, but you never will reach your ultimate destination. Monoculture without diversity of experience, thought, and perspective is a huge liability in business when facing failures or threats, just as it is in agriculture when increasing the risk of failure against diseases or pest outbreaks.

It's not uncommon for companies that are experiencing hypergrowth to hire anyone they can, then throw them into a position and expect them to figure it out. Don't believe that someone will magically go from not knowing what's going on to becoming highly skilled at whatever job you put them in. In most cases, it won't happen. Never put someone who's just learning on the job, and don't jeopardize the mission by expecting instant progress. Don't leave it to chance—hire the best.

The team assembled to design and build the Apple Newton had some of Apple's best and brightest at the time, including Jerome Coonen, software team lead from the original Macintosh team; Steve Capps, a legendary early Mac team engineer; and

Larry Kenyon, who built the networking stack for the original Mac. What they did wasn't magic. All members of the Newton team were recruited specifically for the deep expertise they possessed. They weren't learning on the job—they had already done it and were masters of their craft. Apple didn't leave the development of this groundbreaking new product to chance.

The point is that it's vital to assemble a team that is excellent, world-class at what they do, and not just learning the basics on the job. It's up to you to hire and assemble teams of people who know more than you do and who are top-notch in some aspect of your business, everything from accounting to engineering to sales and much more. Every person you hire should elevate the team and the organization as a whole and should have either the prior experience or the clear potential to scale at the pace your business is scaling. That's how you can set up yourself, your team, and your organization for success—and if you succeed, it will look like magic.

TOLERATE SMALL FAILURES

When you're applying this framework with rigor, you'll find that nothing's ever perfect. There are always going to be failures, mistakes, and missed opportunities. While it's essential to apply the framework, there's also a need to develop a focus on what's most important. The key is not to allow fear of failure to stop the progress of you, your team, and your organization. Failure is going to happen: Anticipate it, and work through it.

I've seen this play out many times in large companies that hire strategy consultants. Smart consultants will come in and tell you at the one hundred thousand–foot level everything that's broken.

To prove their point, they will use data conjured up through benchmarking. More often than not, that creates widespread indecision because everyone suddenly thinks, "Oh my God, how did we go so wrong, and why are we so much worse than everybody else?!" Then you take a bunch of action items, and everybody goes off helter-skelter to fix all the problems, both real and perceived.

Things get better when you focus on the important things. There's a rate at which you can effect change. As an organization gets larger and more complex, the rate at which you can assimilate and propagate change is limited. Therefore, you have to focus on what's important and stage it. You've got to think about the thing that matters most for the business and focus on it.

Dr. Roland Busch could have satisfied the Siemens managing board by making short-term fixes to the rolling stock business that would have quickly improved financial results without addressing the organization's more deep-seated problems. But that is not how Roland proceeded. Instead, after explaining to the managing board that he would need more than just a few quarters to providing lasting results, he focused on diving deep into the biggest problem the business faced: delivering products to customers on time. He then staged the organization's turnaround by setting long-term goals, creating achievable budgets that continuously raised the bar, and improving morale.

In addition, you have to be ready to tolerate a certain amount of failure. You can't afford to get into so many battles that you lose sight of your destination or that your team or organization becomes paralyzed. If you want to keep moving forward—and you do—you've got to accept that things are never going to be perfect and build tolerance for small failures into the organization and within yourself.

There's one more thing about tolerating small failures to consider. If you don't tolerate them, if you punish or berate or yell at people who bring them to you, then people are going to stop reporting them. People will refrain from admitting bad news or accepting that they failed to any degree. As a result, you're going to create an organization that soon will fall apart because of a lack of tolerance for failures.

Create an environment where it is safe to fail—where people pick themselves up, learn from their mistakes, and try again. By keeping your eye on the priorities, avoiding too much entropy in the system, and creating an organization where it is safe to fail, you will be in a better position to avoid catastrophic failures.

Although it may make you uncomfortable in the beginning, it's important to make failures transparent and celebrate them when they happen, so people know that you mean what you say. If you're not having small failures, then you're not taking enough risk. As Ned Hooper, the head of corporate development when I was at Cisco, used to say, "If a few of your acquisitions are not failing, then you're not taking enough risk." Failures are the sign of an organization that is taking healthy risks and is intellectually honest. In the perilous waters of acquisitions and venture investments, for instance, anyone claiming to be 100 percent successful is not moored to reality, and is certainly not encouraging their team to surface small failures.

BEFORE YOU GO

I opened this book with an excerpt from a song that has special meaning to me. I would like to end this book with another song excerpt that in just a handful of words encapsulates for me how anticipating failure and working through it will bring us all the success we seek in business and in life. The song, *"Rote Hue Aate Hain Sab,"* is from the popular 1978 film *Muqaddar Ka Sikandar,* featuring the undisputed king of Hindi cinema, Amitabh Bachchan. The lyrics go like this:

> *Everyone comes crying*
> *But the one who will smile when he leaves*
> *He will be called the king of destiny*

While these lyrics originally were meant to describe the circle of life—our birth and death, and the journey and choices we make in between—I believe they also can be considered in a business-building context. My interpretation of these words is that all founders face failure from the moment their venture is born, but those who anticipate failure and turn it into success at the end of their journey will be the rulers of their destiny.

As founders, CEOs, and executives, we have the great opportunity to bring new businesses to life and to take our people, our customers, our communities, and our investors on remarkable journeys along the way to our ultimate success. People want to work for great organizations, with other talented and motivated people, and customers want to buy products they love, built by companies that share their ideals and values.

It's up to you to create these great organizations, to build products that people love, and to deliver the future. Whenever I hear a founder's pitch for a promising new product or startup, I can't help but be amazed by the seemingly limitless universe of opportunities out there waiting to be discovered, developed, and put into the hands of people who need them. I am deeply grateful to be in this position that allows me a peek into the truly incredible future that awaits us all.

I hope that in the pages of this book, you have gained the tools you need to become the ruler of your own destiny. If you have, then my own dream will have been realized through your success.

ENDNOTES

1   https://www.businesswire.com/news/home/20180807005288/en/WndrCo-Announces-Initial-Capital-Raise-of-1-Billion-for-New-Media-Platform

2   https://www.wsj.com/articles/alibaba-hollywood-studios-are-among-those-pouring-1-billion-into-a-mobile-video-startup-1533636000

3   https://www.statista.com/statistics/330695/number-of-smartphone-users-worldwide/

4   https://www.businesswire.com/news/home/20180807005288/en/WndrCo-Announces-Initial-Capital-Raise-of-1-Billion-for-New-Media-Platform

5   https://www.wndrco.com/portfolio/quibi/

6   https://thelongandshort.org/enterprise/how-the-beatles-revolutionised-medical-imaging

7   https://www.theverge.com/2018/9/20/17878676/electric-scooter-bird-lime-uber-lyft

8   https://www.mckinsey.com/industries/automotive-and-assembly/our-insights/the-future-of-micromobility-ridership-and-revenue-after-a-crisis

9   https://www.sba.gov/sites/default/files/advocacy/Frequently-Asked-Questions-Small-Business-2018.pdf

10 https://www.innosight.com/insight/creative-destruction/

11 https://dev-meetingsmeanbusiness.pantheonsite.io/sites/default/files/Economic%20Significance%20of%20Meetings%20to%20the%20US%20Economy.pdf

12 https://www.crunchbase.com/organization/bizzabo/company_financials

13 https://www.globenewswire.com/news-release/2020/12/02/2138280/0/en/Bizzabo-Raises-138-Million-to-Power-the-Hybrid-Future-of-Professional-Events.html

14 https://www.dw.com/en/tata-nano-end-of-the-road-for-worlds-cheapest-car/a-45427649

15 https://www.businesstoday.in/current/economy-politics/how-a-scooter-on-a-rainy-day-turned-into-ratan-tatas-dream-project-nano/story/239035.html

16 Kevin Freiberg, Jackie Freiberg, and Dain Dunston, *Nanovation: How a Little Car Can Teach the World to Think Big & Act Bold*, Thomas Nelson (2011) p. 8

17 https://www.businesstoday.in/current/economy-politics/how-a-scooter-on-a-rainy-day-turned-into-ratan-tatas-dream-project-nano/story/239035.html

18 https://bengaluru.citizenmatters.in/some-lessons-for-bengaluru-from-100-years-of-rain-data-8013

19 https://www.statista.com/statistics/749669/india-fatal-road-accidents-by-type-of-vehicle/

20 https://databank.worldbank.org/data/download/poverty/987B9C90-CB9F-4D93-AE8C-750588BF00QA/AM2020/Global_POVEQ_IND.pdf

21 https://wheels.blogs.nytimes.com/2008/01/10/tata-nano-the-worlds-cheapest-car/

22 https://www.financialexpress.com/auto/car-news/tata-ace-indias-first-mini-truck-crosses-two-million-sales-in-12-yrs/981502/

23 Kevin Freiberg, Jackie Freiberg, and Dain Dunston, *Nanovation: How a Little Car Can Teach the World to Think Big & Act Bold*, Thomas Nelson (2011) p. 81

24   https://www.bbc.com/news/world-south-asia-11726992

25   http://www.globalncap.org/tata-nano-offers-zero-star-safety-fails-to-meet-minimum-safety-standards/

26   https://www.just-auto.com/news/loss-making-tata-nano-kept-going-for-emotional-reasons-mistry
      _id172977.aspx

27   https://www.dw.com/en/tata-nano-end-of-the-road-for-worlds-cheapest-car/a-45427649

28   Steve Blank, *The Four Steps to the Epiphany: Successful Strategies for Products That Win*, Wiley (2020) p. 6

29   Steve Blank, *The Four Steps to the Epiphany: Successful Strategies for Products That Win*, Wiley (2020) p. 3

30   https://www.cnn.com/2018/10/30/tech/segway-history/index.html

31   https://www.pcmag.com/opinions/dean-kamen-doesnt-have-450-patents-he-has-way-more

32   https://www.caranddriver.com/features/a15139357/2001-10best-cars-feature/

33   https://www.theledger.com/news/20061017/reinventing-the-wheel

34   https://www.fastcompany.com/90517971/
      exclusive-segway-the-most-hyped-invention-since-the-macintosh-to-end-production

35   http://content.time.com/time/business/article/0,8599,186660,00.html

36   https://youtu.be/Tppv2NgZOQU

37   https://www.wsj.com/articles/SB1037631947739311148

38   https://spectrum.ieee.org/tech-talk/consumer-electronics/gadgets
      /the-segway-is-dead-but-its-technology-and-vision-lives-on

39   https://www.engadget.com/2006-09-14-segway-recalls-all-23-500-scooters-sold-due-to-software-glitch.html

40   https://www.theledger.com/news/20061017/reinventing-the-wheel

41   https://techcrunch.com/2019/06/07/a-peek-inside-sequoia-capitals-low-flying-wide-reaching-scout
      -program/

42   https://www.businessofapps.com/data/uber-statistics/

43   https://investor.uber.com/home/default.aspx

44   Ron Adner, *The Wide Lens: What Successful Innovators See That Others Miss*, Portfolio/Penguin (2013)
      pp. 2-3

45   Ron Adner, *The Wide Lens: What Successful Innovators See That Others Miss*, Portfolio/Penguin (2013)
      pp. 4-5

46   Ron Adner, *The Wide Lens: What Successful Innovators See That Others Miss*, Portfolio/Penguin (2013) p. 7

47   https://hbswk.hbs.edu/archive/steve-jobs-and-jeff-bezos-meet-ginger

48   https://escholarship.org/uc/item/00m5410t

49   https://www.precisely.com/blog/mainframe/mainframe-still-matters

50   https://www.blackwellpublishing.com/content/GrantContemporaryStrategyAnalysis/docs/Grant_Cases
      _Guide_Chapter_10.pdf

51   https://www.blackwellpublishing.com/content/GrantContemporaryStrategyAnalysis/docs/Grant_Cases
      _Guide_Chapter_10.pdf

52   https://zephoria.com/top-15-valuable-facebook-statistics

53   https://www.macworld.com/article/3019878/15-years-of-itunes-a-look-at-apples-media-app-and-its
      -influence-on-an-industry.html

54   https://www.poynter.org/reporting-editing/2014
      /today-in-media-history-apples-steve-jobs-introduces-the-ipod-in-2001

55   https://www.cultofmac.com/539643/100-million-ipods-sold/

56   https://en.wikipedia.org/wiki/ITunes_Store

57   https://www.nobelprize.org/prizes/economic-sciences/1990/sharpe/facts/

58   https://connect.mmc.com/BenefitsFormsDocuments/DC_Your%20Guide%20to%20Financial%20
      Engines.pdf

59   https://www.roboadvisorpros.com/robo-advisors-with-most-aum-assets-under-management/

60   https://www.canalys.com/newsroom/global-cloud-market-q4-2020

61   Interview: Jeff Bezos and David Rubenstein, The Economic Club of Washington, D.C., September 13, 2018
     https://youtu.be/zN1PyNwjHpc

62   https://www.cnet.com/news/oracles-ellison-nails-cloud-computing/

63   https://www.networkworld.com/article/2160175/once-a-basher--now-a-believer--oracle-chief-larry
     -ellison-has-come-full-circle-on-cl.html

64   https://youtu.be/oeqPrUmVz-o

65   https://www.tesla.com/blog/secret-tesla-motors-master-plan-just-between-you-and-me

66   https://cleantechnica.com/2020/01/19/tesla-model-3-7th-best-selling-car-in-usa/

67   https://carsalesbase.com/us-bmw-3-series/

68   https://insideevs.com/news/487969/2020-us-electric-car-sales-tesla-share/

69   https://www.engadget.com/2013-01-30-facebook-2012-q4-earnings.html

70   http://content.time.com/time/magazine/article/0,9171,32207-5,00.html

71   https://www.cnbc.com/2020/09/16/snowflake-snow-opening-trading-on-the-nyse.html

72   https://www.pro-football-reference.com/coaches/WalsBi0.htm

73   https://hbr.org/1993/01/to-build-a-winning-team-an-interview-with-head-coach-bill-walsh

74   https://www.emeraldgrouppublishing.com/archived/learning/management_thinking/interviews/hansen.htm

75   https://hbr.org/2020/11/how-apple-is-organized-for-innovation

76   https://www.idc.com/promo/smartphone-market-share/os

77   https://venturebeat.com/2010/10/27/google-exec-android-was-best-deal-ever/

78   https://www.theverge.com/2019/5/7/18528297
     /google-io-2019-android-devices-play-store-total-number-statistic-keynote

79   https://www.cnet.com/reviews/essential-phone-ph-1-review/

80   https://www.theverge.com/circuitbreaker/2017/8/14/16142772
     /andy-rubin-essential-phone-valuation-billion-dollars-unicorn-value

81   https://www.cnet.com/reviews/essential-phone-ph-1-review/

82   https://www.androidauthority.com/essential-phone-5000-sold-803111/

83   https://techcrunch.com/2018/02/12/essential-reportedly-only-shipped-88000-phones-in-2017/

84   https://www.theverge.com/2020/2/12/21134985/essential-phone-shutting-down-andy-rubin-startup

85   https://lowendmac.com/2013/the-story-behind-apples-newton/

86   https://www.cultofmac.com/500178/apple-history-steve-jobs-kills-newton/

87   https://www.cultofmac.com/469567/today-in-apple-history-apple-bids-farewell-to-the-newton/

88   https://www.zdnet.com/article/you-can-buy-a-new-iphone-for-less-than-the-original-palmpilot/

89   https://www.cnet.com/news/palmpilot-continues-winning-ways/

90   https://www.statista.com/chart/19058/how-many-websites-are-there/

91   https://www.inc.com/carmine-gallo/how-former-cisco-ceo-john-chambers-instantly-builds-rapport-with
     -everyone-he-meets.html

92   https://hbr.org/2008/11/cisco-sees-the-future

93   https://hbr.org/2008/11/cisco-sees-the-future

94   https://www.cnbc.com/2019/09/24/facebook-bought-instagram-because-it-was-scared-of-twitter-and
     -google.html

95   https://www.reuters.com/article/us-mobike-m-a-meituan
     /chinas-meituan-dianping-acquires-bike-sharing-firm-mobike-for-2-7-billion-idUSKCN1HB0DU

96   https://www.theverge.com/2018/9/20/17878676/electric-scooter-bird-lime-uber-lyft

97   https://www.mckinsey.com/industries/automotive-and-assembly/our-insights
     /the-future-of-micromobility-ridership-and-revenue-after-a-crisis

98   https://www.mckinsey.com/industries/automotive-and-assembly/our-insights
     /the-future-of-micromobility-ridership-and-revenue-after-a-crisis

99   https://micromobility.io/blog/2018/12/7/the-bull-case-for-micromobility

100 https://www.nbcnews.com/id/wbna39332696

101 https://www.digitalcommerce360.com/2020/05/26
     /amazon-is-the-fourth%E2%80%91largest-us-delivery-service-and-growing-fast/

102 https://www.washingtonpost.com/technology/2020/11/27/amazon-shipping-competitive-threat/

103 https://www.washingtonpost.com/technology/2020/11/27/amazon-shipping-competitive-threat/

104 https://www.verkada.com/about/

105 Filip's approach to decision-making is similar to what is known as the Eisenhower matrix, where the
     vertical axis is a task's importance, and the horizontal axis is a task's urgency. The Eisenhower matrix is
     attributed to a speech given by Dwight D. Eisenhower in 1954 on the campus of Northwestern University in
     Evanston, Illinois. He said, "I have two kinds of problems, the urgent and the important. The urgent are not
     important, and the important are never urgent."

106 https://press.siemens.com/global/en/pressrelease/earnings-release-and-financial-results-q4-fy-2020

107 https://www.washingtonpost.com/technology/2020/11/27/amazon-shipping-competitive-threat/

108 https://www.cnet.com/news/take-a-trip-down-memory-lane-to-googles-first-data-center/

109 https://www.datacenterknowledge.com/archives/2014/07/23
     /from-112-servers-to-5b-spent-on-google-data-centers-per-quarter

ACKNOWLEDGMENTS

Many people played a role in this book, and I would like to give each one of you my sincere thanks.

I must start with my family.

To my wife, Preethi: You are my biggest supporter, and I am grateful that I can count on you to be on my side in all of my endeavors, and for your unflinching love and moral support.

To my son, Jayanth: You are my greatest joy in life. You inspire me to be the best I can be as a father. I hope that you will always carry a part of me in you, and that you find yourself as you grow up.

To my father and mother, B. Ananthapadmanabhan and A. Saroja: You have been the rock I can always depend on throughout my life. I am eternally grateful to you for your selflessness and sacrifices to give me everything I have since the day I was born.

And to the rest of my extended family—uncles, aunts, cousins, grandparents who have passed away, in-laws, nieces, nephews, and everyone else. I am blessed to be born into this family where everyone has always encouraged me, cheered me on, and shared their heartfelt joy in my successes big and small.

I would like to thank the many contributors to this book—it simply would not exist without your help.

To my co-writer Peter Economy for assimilating my ideas and presenting them so elegantly in this book. Our collaboration during the book-writing journey was very enjoyable—thank you for making it so.

To Matthew Cowan, T. J. Rylander, Ching-Yu Hu, and Sabrina Guttman at Next47: Your ideas, reviews, support, and thought partnership made this book better.

And to all the remarkable people who so graciously agreed to be interviewed for this book, including Eran Ben-Shushan, CEO, Bizzabo; Dr. Roland Busch, President and CEO, Siemens AG; Matthew Cowan, General Partner, Next47; Kevin Freiberg, Co-founder, Epic Work Epic Life; Andre Hartung, President of Diagnostic Imaging at Siemens Healthineers; Ching-Yu Hu, Partner, Next47; James Joaquin, Co-founder and Managing Director of Obvious Ventures; Filip Kaliszan, CEO, Verkada; Li Pu, Founder, A4X; Gokul Rajaram, Executive Team, DoorDash; and Hans Robertson, Executive Chairman, Verkada.

Several people served as inspirations for this book.

First and foremost, to Dr. Roland Busch: Your aspirational vision, optimism, strong work ethic, and genuine care for people is a living model of what every truly great leader can be. Your support for Next47 made this book possible.

To Ron Adner: I'm grateful to have had the opportunity to be a student in your class. Not only did you inspire me to tackle the topic of failure in this book, but I also owe the book's title to you. I use what I learned in your class every day.

To Meg Whitman: Thank you for giving me the opportunity to create Hewlett Packard Pathfinder, which brought to life my ideas on building a top-tier venture group backed by a great corporation. And thank you for trusting me to work with you as you turned around HP from a very perilous position. I learned so much from you about leadership, strategy, people, and communications.

And to all the founders—past, present, and future—who chose or will choose to work with my team at Next47. Your vision, passion, and unbelievable ability to turn vision into reality give me the greatest professional inspiration and satisfaction.

I would also like to thank my colleagues at Next47 and Siemens. I'm amazed at what we have created together and thrilled for our future as we continue to build an amazing, global venture firm that the best founders in the world choose to partner with.

And I would be remiss if I neglected to mention a few other people who have played important roles in my life.

To N. Kumar—respected entrepreneur, leader in Indian industry, and fellow board member at Mphasis—for your kindness, humility, and inspiration for what can be achieved in a great career as a business leader.

To Dr. Medhat Morcos, Professor Emeritus, Kansas State University: You called my home in India in 1994, encouraged me to come to Kansas State University, and promised me that you would take care of me. And you did—from offering me a research assistantship to paying my first-semester tuition to always looking out for my welfare—in addition to inspiring me to do great academic work.

To Phil Wickham, Managing Director, Sozo Ventures, for inculcating the values of the Kauffman Fellows by being a living example. You have offered invaluable career advice every time I needed it.

To Mark Thornton, former Partner at 3i, for giving me a break as an Associate with 3i in Singapore and launching my career in investment. You saw the potential in me and looked beyond my credentials on paper.

To Cisco Corporate Development: Thanks to all the members of the Corporate Development team at Cisco who collectively taught me how to operate in the big leagues of technology acquisitions and investments.

ABOUT THE AUTHOR

Lak Ananth is an Indian American venture capitalist who thrives on identifying industry-changing disruptions and acts on them as an investor in close collaboration with founders. Lak is the CEO and Managing Partner of the global venture capital firm Next47 which is backed by Siemens AG. Next47 partners with visionary founders from around the globe and serves them as they build companies that will profoundly advance how the world works.

Lak has spent his career in service to the entrepreneurial pursuit. In addition to running Next47, he serves on the board of several companies that he has helped to grow beyond $1B valuations. As an investor and board member, Lak believes in establishing mutual trust with founders so when key decisions need to be made, he can provide thoughtful counsel in anticipating failure modes and seizing opportunities instrumental to success.

Lak holds an MBA from INSEAD and The Wharton School of Business, and he earned graduate and undergraduate degrees in electrical engineering. He is also a Kauffman Fellow.

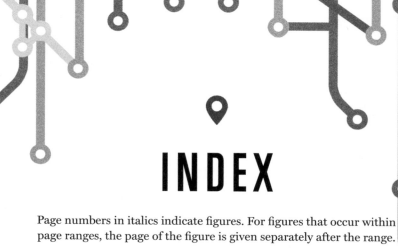

INDEX

Page numbers in italics indicate figures. For figures that occur within page ranges, the page of the figure is given separately after the range.

D

Danger, Inc., 109
Danger Hiptop smartphone
(Sidekick), 109
Data
following, 68, 82–84, 127–128
incomplete, 178, 181
misuse, 185–186
timing and, 118–122
Decision-making, 155, 160, 174–
175, 178
Delegating, 161
Destinations for business models,
180
Diamond Multimedia (digital
music), 68
Differentiation, 110, 144–146,
149–151
Digital music, 68–71
Discovery of customers, 31–32, 34,
39–40
Diversity, 105, 180, 190
DJI (drones), 128
DoorDash, 81
Dosti (film), 1
DreamWorks, 9
Drones, 128–129

E

Early adopters vs. majority, 36, 46,
78–79, 143, 149
Eastman Kodak, 175
eBay, 9–10, 129, 188
Ecosystems
developing, 70, 108, 115
new technology and, 49–51,
52–56, 59
Uber, 47–49
unit economics and, 140–141
Einstein, Albert, 21
Elastic Compute Cloud (EC2), 73.
See also Amazon Web Services
Electric bicycles, 57
Ellison, Larry, 75, 125
EMI (Electric and Musical
Industries, Ltd.), 13, 61–62,
63–64

Essential Phone, 108–109, 110–112,
120
Evolution, continuous
Bizzabo, 19
CT scanners, 64–66
Facebook, 68, 80–81, 84
iPod, 70
market requirements and, 58
Execution. *See also* incumbents;
Siemens AG; Verkada
Amazon, 153–155
aspects of, 173–175
competing with Goliaths, 158,
175–176
failure of, 32–33, 153
hiring your betters, 95, 104,
159–161
importance of, 172–173
limits of, 52
premature, 36
risks, *54*
speed, 174
Exodus co-location space, 188
Experience, necessity of, 96, 103–
104, 190–191

F

Facebook, 68, 80–81, 82–84, 127–
128, 185–186
Failures. *See also more specifics
under each type of failure*
business model, 131–151
commonness of, 7–22
customer, 23–40
execution, 153–176
patterns of, 15
product, 61–84
team, 85–105
technology, 41–59
timing, 107–130
transforming into success,
177–195
Fairchild Semiconductor, 93–94
Fast followers, 13, 72–73, 79, 81
FedEx, 154
Feedback cycles, 18, 79–80, 82–84,
174, 183